LEBANESE
FOOD & COOKING

LEBANESE
FOOD & COOKING

traditions • ingredients • tastes • techniques • 80 classic recipes

Ghillie Başan

with photographs by Jon Whitaker

aqua marine

This edition is published by Aquamarine, an imprint of Anness Publishing Ltd, Hermes House, 88–89 Blackfriars Road, London SE1 8HA; tel. 020 7401 2077; fax 020 7633 9499

www.aquamarinebooks.com; www.annesspublishing.com

If you like the images in this book and would like to investigate using them for publishing, promotions or advertising, please visit our website www.practicalpictures.com for more information.

UK agent: The Manning Partnership Ltd; tel. 01225 478444; fax 01225 478440; sales@manning-partnership.co.uk
UK distributor: Grantham Book Services Ltd; tel. 01476 541080; fax 01476 541061; orders@gbs.tbs-ltd.co.uk
North American agent/distributor: National Book Network; tel. 301 459 3366; fax 301 429 5746; www.nbnbooks.com
Australian agent/distributor: Pan Macmillan Australia; tel. 1300 135 113; fax 1300 135 103; customer.service@macmillan.com.au
New Zealand agent/distributor: David Bateman Ltd; tel. (09) 415 7664; fax (09) 415 8892

Publisher: Joanna Lorenz
Editorial Director: Helen Sudell
Executive Editor: Joanne Rippin
Designer: Adelle Morris
Photography: Jon Whitaker
Food Stylist: Fergal Connelly
Prop Stylist: Helen Trent
Production Controller: Wendy Lawson

ETHICAL TRADING POLICY

Because of our ongoing ecological investment programme, you, as our customer, can have the pleasure and reassurance of knowing that a tree is being cultivated on your behalf to naturally replace the materials used to make the book you are holding. For further information about this scheme, go to www.annesspublishing.com/trees.

NOTES

Bracketed terms are intended for American readers.
For all recipes, quantities are given in both metric and imperial measures and, where appropriate, in standard cups and spoons. Follow one set of measures, but not a mixture, because they are not interchangeable.

Standard spoon and cup measures are level. 1 tsp = 5ml, 1 tbsp = 15ml, 1 cup = 250ml/8fl oz.
Australian standard tablespoons are 20ml. Australian readers should use 3 tsp in place of 1 tbsp for measuring small quantities.
American pints are 16fl oz/2 cups. American readers should use 20fl oz/2.5 cups in place of 1 pint when measuring liquids.
Electric oven temperatures in this book are for conventional ovens. When using a fan oven, the temperature will probably need to be reduced by about 10–20°C/20–40°F. Since ovens vary, you should check with your manufacturer's instruction book for guidance.
The nutritional analysis given for each recipe is calculated per portion (i.e. serving or item), unless otherwise stated. If the recipe gives a range, such as Serves 4–6, then the nutritional analysis will be for the smaller portion size, i.e. 6 servings. Measurements for sodium do not include salt added to taste. Medium (US large) eggs are used unless otherwise stated.

Front cover shows Cream cheese pudding with syrup and nuts – for recipe, see page 144

PUBLISHER'S NOTE: Although the advice and information in this book are believed to be accurate and true at the time of going to press, neither the authors nor the publisher can accept any legal responsibility or liability for any errors or omissions that may be made.

Contents

Landscape and geography

Although a small country, Lebanon boasts a vibrant cuisine, richly influenced by its climate and geography. A narrow coastal strip winds its way along the edge of the warm Mediterranean, with high mountains rising to the east, behind which lies the fertile Bekaa Valley, the main source of much of Lebanon's food. Sea, mountains and sheltered valley are all within a few miles of each other, and all play a part in the country's distinctive food culture.

A varied landscape

Lebanon divides quite naturally into four main regions, all running from north to south. Along the coast, a mere 3 kilometres/1.8 miles of flat terrain gives just enough space for the major towns to gain a foothold before the mountains begin to climb towards the sky. These ports became important trading centres in the early medieval period, dealing in all kinds of foodstuffs. There is also a little room on the coastal strip for growing tender vegetables and fruit, particularly citrus fruit, with orchards and fields packed into this small fertile space.

As the Lebanon Mountains rise, the terraced lower slopes sprout almond and olive trees bathed in the warm sunshine. The mountain peaks rise to over 3,300m (11,000ft) in the north of the range and most are topped with snow throughout the year. Trading across the mountains was a risky enterprise hundreds of years ago, but now routes are well established.

The third main geographical area in Lebanon is the fantastically productive Bekaa Valley, nestled between the Lebanon Mountains to the west and the Anti-Lebanon mountains to the east. This is a valley rich in agriculture of all kinds, from settled farming to nomadic herding, that has changed little over the centuries. Lastly, the Anti-Lebanon Mountains protect the Bekaa Valley from the heat of the deserts. The highest peaks of these

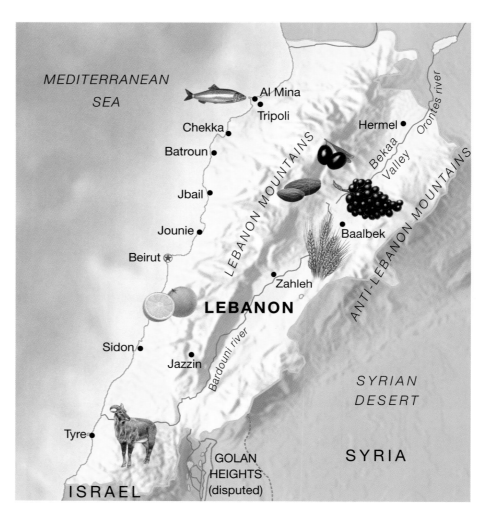

mountains, like those of the Lebanon Mountains, are snow-covered for much of the year. This area is more thinly populated than the western side of the country, with fewer farms and other businesses, and the border with Syria snakes along the top of the range.

Above: Lebanon is divided into three main areas: coast, mountains and fertile valley.

A benign climate

Lebanon is fortunate in having a perfect climate for growing many crops. In the lowlands, the summers are long and hot, but the winters mild and rainy, allowing the ground to recover its fertility. The coastal strip is hot and dry, but heavy dew is often formed during the night to keep the fruit and vegetables watered. Many Lebanese escape from the coast to the mountains during the summer, and there are several beautiful resorts with splendid hotels and restaurants catering for both locals and tourists. Parallel to the Bekaa Valley is the northenmost seaside resort, the ancient town of Al Mina, once a Phoenician port, and now known for its fried fish. On the other side of the mountains, the Bekaa Valley receives warm sunshine to ripen summer crops, but can also experience very cold, biting winds during the winter, whistling down from the north between the two mountain ranges.

The Middle East food bowl

Lebanon was once a principal provider of grain to Imperial Rome, and many of the subsequent occupying powers have coveted the fruits of its fertile soil. The landscape of the grain-growing regions of central Lebanon has changed little for hundreds of years. The land is still tilled by oxen, and groups of peasants work in the fields. Orchards of peaches, apricots and pomegranates, and small vineyards often surround the villages. Young boys tend the goats or sheep while the women thresh the wheat or grind the corn. There is as much culinary activity on the flat roofs as there is indoors, as they provide an ideal surface for fruit and corn to dry in the sun alongside flat trays of tomatoes and bell peppers.

Renowned for its fresh air and natural springs, the Bekaa Valley has been productive for centuries. The valley's capital is Zahleh. Under French influence this picturesque town became known for its cafés and restaurants, which set a trend copied by other riverside towns and coastal resorts, where open-air restaurants sprang up along the river and beach promenades.

Above: Fishing is still an important part of life in Lebanon's coastal towns.

The valley acts as a temporary home for groups of Bedouin migrating from the hot Syrian desert in the springtime each year. Here they set up their goat-hair tents and graze their Awassi sheep, prized for the fat stored in their tails.

Below: A view of the spectacular Bekaa Valley, with vineyards in the foreground. This is Lebanon's most fertile farming land.

About this book Lebanon's vibrant mix of culinary traditions is celebrated in this book of easy-to-follow recipes for traditional dishes. The first three chapters give instructions for delicious mezze, salads, soups and hot snacks. Then follows a chapter on grains and pulses, with fragrant pilaffs that are the centrepiece of Lebanese hospitality. Chapters that highlight Lebanon's love of tangy fish, sizzling meat, vegetables and preserves are followed by a chapter of scented desserts and sweetmeats. Together these chapters present an evocative collection of appetizing Lebanese recipes to suit all occasions.

Historical perspective

Lebanese cooking is reputed to be one of the most refined cuisines in the world. It is very similar to that of Turkey, with distinct culinary elements from Syria and Jordan. All these countries were united within the Golden Age of Islam and the Ottoman Empire. Lebanon has developed an all-embracing cuisine that has absorbed many influences throughout its long history of invasion and foreign rule, and made them part of its own food culture.

The classical period

Lebanon, Syria, Palestine and Jordan were once part of Greater Syria and, along with Iraq, are located in a part of the eastern Mediterranean that was known as the 'Fertile Crescent', where the soil is rich and the landscape and climate allowed human civilization to flourish. Over 4,000 years ago, the Canaanites came to the area now known as Lebanon and settled in the city-states of Tyre, Sidon and Byblos. The Greeks referred to the Canaanites as Phoenicians and, to this day, many Lebanese proudly call themselves Phoenicians, attributing their entrepreneurial acumen to their trading ancestors. The Phoenicians were a seafaring people, launching cargo vessels along the African and European coasts, and dominating the Mediterranean as they created coastal colonies and opened up the trade routes. In due course the Phoenicians were conquered by the Assyrians. The Assyrians were followed in their turn by a series of invaders and conquerors, including the Babylonians, Persians, Macedonians, Romans, Byzantines, Arab Caliphs, Crusaders, Egyptian Mamelukes (who had risen to power from their origins as slave soldiers to their Egyptian masters) and finally the Ottoman Turks, who seized Greater Syria in 1517 and ruled for the next 400 years.

New traditions and ingredients

Throughout its history, each successive occupation left its legacy on the region's increasingly rich and complex culture: in its architecture, in its religion, and most notably in its cuisine. The Byzantine Empire brought the culinary customs of Christian orthodoxy, which forbade eating meat or fish and drinking milk or wine during Lent and other fast days, while the arrival of Islam imposed new religious restrictions on the preparation of meat and the consumption of alcohol.

The Ottoman Turks wielded the greatest influence of all, appointing local feudal lords as governors of each state and imposing their own food culture. In the 16th and 17th centuries, the Ottoman Empire became so vast and powerful that it dominated the world stage. As Spanish explorers opened up the New World, they were induced to stop off along the North African coast with the goods they brought back, and ingredients such as chilli peppers,

Below: The city of Tyre was first settled 4,000 years ago, and has prospered as a trading centre throughout the centuries.

tomatoes and maize were distributed throughout the empire, altering and enhancing the character of the whole region's cuisine.

A French colony

When the Ottoman Empire finally collapsed at the end of World War I, the League of Nations awarded France the mandate for Syria and Mount Lebanon. The French occupation of Lebanon from 1920 to 1946 introduced the sophisticated style and elegance of France to its cuisine as well as to other aspects of its culture, while the new colony enchanted the French with its diversity and wealth of opportunity. Soon Lebanon became known among wealthy businessmen and jetsetters as a fashionable place to be. With its reputation in the Middle East as a centre

Above: This elevated view of modern Lebanon shows the central Hamra district of the reconstructed city of Beirut.

Below: The impressive Roman ruins of the temple to Bacchus in Baalbek are thought to be the best-preserved in the world.

for international business and a tourist haven, Beirut soon established itself as a food connoisseur's paradise with a touch of French elegance.

An independent state

In 1946, Lebanon gained its independence and was free of foreign rule for the first time for many centuries. But there was to be no easy path to freedom: the proximity of Israel and Syria ensured that the next few years were turbulent and it was difficult to establish and stabilize the much-needed farming and tourist industries. With the partition of Palestine in 1948, a number of refugees fled to Lebanon and Jordan, adding their own food culture to the already varied culinary pool, and more followed throughout the next 50 years, bringing the cooking traditions of their

country. The exhausting civil war in Lebanon of 1975 to 1990 wrecked many new enterprises, especially the hotel and tourist trade; however, even during times of unrest, restaurants in Beirut have been known to remain open, serving exquisite dishes amid the chaos of exploding bombs.

Modern Lebanon

Present-day Lebanon is coming to terms with its new-found stability. A democratic government has been elected and prosperity has returned to many businesses. Lebanese entrepreneurs are proud of their capacity to survive and rebuild. Beirut is returning to normal, with its restaurants beginning to thrive, as is the appetite of locals and visitors for delicious food. Holidaymakers are filling the hotels and fanning out into the delightful countryside, and the Lebanese once more have the time, strength and resources to practise their valued culinary arts.

Feasts and festivals

The Lebanese population is made up of roughly 59 per cent Muslims, 40 per cent Christians and 1 per cent other religions. With a tolerant attitude to the customs and cuisine of all faiths, Lebanon has long been a refuge for people fleeing religious persecution. The culinary year flows from one religious feast to another, incorporating the food traditions of both Muslim and Christian calendars and observing the main feast days of both as national holidays.

Festive enthusiasm

On religious and festive occasions, food and entertainment dominate all walks of life, and whether it is in the cobbled streets of a crumbling village or on the smart Avenue de Paris in Beirut, the cultural activity rises to a frenzy of music and dance, accompanied by mounds of spicy kibbeh, the national dish.

Easter

The most important date of all on the Lebanese Christian calendar is Easter. On Good Friday, when devout Christians

Above: The festival of St Helena's Day, Eid al-Salib, is marked with huge firework displays over Lebanese towns and cities.

Below: Christian Holy Week is marked by processions such as this one in Beirut.

abstain from meat, a variety of vegetable, bean and lentil dishes are eaten, such as mdardara, rice cooked with lentils, and a sour bulgur soup called shoraba zingool. The sourness of this soup is intended to remind Christians of the vinegar offered on a sponge to Christ on the cross by the Roman centurion. On Easter Sunday, large platters of ma'amoul, little semolina cakes stuffed with walnuts or dates, are offered to celebrate the end of Lent, the period of penitence and prayer observed by devout Christian communities.

Eid al-Salib – St Helena's Day

One of the most celebrated feast days among the Christian communities is Eid al-Salib, St Helena's Day, on 8 September. The legend goes that Queen Helena, the Mother of the Roman Emperor

Constantine, discovered the True Cross of the Crucifixion on a hillside above Jerusalem and demanded that fires be lit in watchtowers all the way to Constantinople to spread the news. To commemorate this historical legend in Lebanon, fires are lit, and fireworks light up the sky as Christians, and Muslims too, gather to dance and feast in the open air, and street vendors sell kibbeh and other delights late into the night.

Ramadan

The vast majority of the population of Lebanon is Muslim, and therefore the month of Ramadan (usually in

September) plays an important part in the region's religious year. This is the month when all Muslims fast between sunrise and sunset to mark the time when Muhammad experienced the revelation of the Qur'an. This means that the first meal of the day, suhur, is prepared before dawn and is designed to fill the belly for the daylight hours of fasting ahead, so it normally comprises a hearty soup and bread. Itfar, the second and last meal of the day that is consumed once the sun has gone down, is much more extensive, involving savoury pastries, meatballs or kibbeh, stuffed vegetables, and numerous sweet dishes, such as baklava, milk puddings, fruit compotes, and ma'amoul, little semolina cakes. Drinks such as sherbets made from carob and tamarind are served to accompany dishes of roasted lamb and chicken with rice, and dates are always placed on the table at religious feasts to serve as a reminder that they were the only source of food for the Prophet Mohammad when he was fasting in the desert. The purpose of Ramadan is to teach self-discipline, which is a necessary virtue when submitting to the will of God, and to instil compassion for the poor who experience hunger all year round.

Eid al-Fitr

Once the month of Ramadan comes to an end, it is time to celebrate with a great deal of merriment and feasting over a three-day period. This joyful holiday is called Eid al-Fitr, and it marks a time when people exchange gifts, buy new clothes, and visit relatives and friends. Two public holidays are set aside for Eid al-Fitr to allow everyone to eat and drink whatever they like, making up for the previous month of restraint.

Eid el-Barbara

Another Christian celebration that Muslims also enjoy in Lebanon is Eid el-Barbara, which marks the end of the harvest in late November. In a similar fashion to the Western traditions of Halloween, the children dress up, wear masks and devour sweet treats.

Left: The meal eaten at the end of the day during Ramadan will finish with a delicious array of sweet pastries.

In Lebanon the traditional treat consists of bowls of kamhiyeh, wheat or barley sweetened with sugar and decorated with pomegranate seeds.

Christmas

At Christmas Christian communities in Lebanon generally celebrate with an exchange of gifts and a celebration family meal of roasted bird, or a leg of lamb, on 25 December -- just as Christians do in other parts of the world. The exceptions are the Armenians, who celebrate Christmas on 6 January, the Epiphany, with mounds of sticky awamat, deep-fried fritters bathed in honey or in a scented syrup. Both days are public holidays so that everyone can enjoy a day off.

Below: Flag-festooned food stalls make an appearance at most Lebanese festivals, such as this one selling corn on the cob.

Lebanese cuisine

The cooking of Lebanon, Syria and Jordan is generally regarded as Arab food at its best. Many dishes have their roots in pre-medieval times, and while there are significant differences between eating habits in the countryside and the modern cities, the ancient Lebanese tradition of hospitality is still expressed in a complex and exciting culinary culture.

Town and country traditions

The food of Lebanon has its roots in two traditions: the peasant cooking of its fertile valleys and mountains, and the foreign influences found in the main cities along the coast. Much of the sophistication of town cuisine can be attributed to the influence of the Ottoman Empire. More recently, the French introduced a few of their own specialities but their legacy is more noticeable in the presentation of the food and the quality of service. In the villages of inland Lebanon, ancient ways of preparing food are as they have been for centuries, with an emphasis on good quality food carefully cooked.

Lebanese hospitality

The Arab and Turkish traditions of hospitality and kindness are deeply ingrained in the psyches of most of the region's population, especially the nomadic Bedouin, the people who have the least to give. Over the last few centuries, writers and travellers have commented on the gracious hospitality of a people whose nomadic life has barely changed with the passing of time.

All Lebanese still respect the family values and religious ceremonies and are deeply courteous and hospitable, falling back on their ancient roots at appropriate moments. Hospices, guest-houses, and private homes have provided free food and shelter for travellers throughout the region's history and they still do to this day. When a host welcomes a guest it is normal to hear the words '*bayti, baytak*' ('my house is your house') and usually it is sincerely meant. It is polite to offer food and drink to strangers and to invite

Below: Bedouin women still cook in the same way as they have for generations.

Below: A contemporary Lebanese family meet for the traditional Sunday lunch.

guests to partake in a meal. It is also polite to offer a guest the best cuts of meat, which may include the eyeball, brains or testicles, and it is impolite to refuse! At parties, great mounds of food are consumed, which can be difficult for a Westerner but it is acceptable to leave some on your plate, thus proving to the hostess that she has done her duty and provided you with more than enough.

Eating customs

In most households, apart from the wealthier Westernized families, meals are generally eaten on the floor, often with everyone seated on cushions and gathered around trays that are sometimes raised off the ground. In some traditional families the grandparents may be served in one room with the male head of the house while the women eat with the children, and, in other households, the women and men may eat separately. This is not necessarily for fundamentalist religious reasons as, in some areas, eating separately has simply been a family tradition. In more modern households, though, all the members of the family and their guests eat together.

Lebanon's national dish

Kibbeh is often regarded as the national dish of Lebanon, although it is just as popular in Syria, and the Jordanians, who call it kubba, enjoy it too. The origins of kibbeh are ancient, possibly dating back to Mesopotamia, and the word itself is derived from the Arabic verb meaning 'to form a lump or ball'. A versatile mixture, with endless variations, it is most commonly a combination of minced (ground) lamb and bulgur wheat with grated onion and a variety of herbs and spices, but beef can also be used

Above: No Lebanese market will be without a stall selling huge bowls of spices.

and some Armenians make it with pork. There are also meatless versions employing lentils, vegetables or fish.

The pounding and shaping of traditional kibbeh requires practice and patience, as well as a degree of strength if using the stone mortar and heavy wooden pestle. When you are invited into a Lebanese home, kibbeh is the traditional offering of hospitality. It is also cooked for special occasions.

Cooking methods and utensils

A selection of copper pots, urns and ladles is indispensable in any Lebanese kitchen. The largest copper pot, a *dist*, is tin-lined and supported by two handles as it is often heavy; it will hold a thick soup, a large rice or bulgur pilaff, or it may be used to make a batch of tomato paste, jam, or a fruit molasses. A frying pan, *miqla*, is another important utensil, and a circular metal tray with raised sides is required for savoury and sweet pastries and for oven-baked kibbeh.

A charcoal barbecue, *manqal*, made of clay or metal, is used for cooking meat and fish – this can be a permanent fixture in the kitchen or backyard, or a portable model for use in the garden and in the countryside for picnics.

Food markets

The markets of Lebanon, Syria, Jordan and Turkey played a huge role in the culinary life of the Islamic and Ottoman Empires and are still central to people's lives today. Goods of infinite variety were brought by camel caravan from Arabia, Persia, Armenia, Byzantium, Egypt, India and China and delivered to the markets of Beirut, Aleppo and Constantinople. Today's *suqs*, or markets – from the sprawling cluster of permanent bazaars in the cities to the makeshift stalls of the mountain villages – have a variety and abundance of fresh vegetables and fruit that can be almost overwhelming. The aroma of spices is ever-present, emanating from the spice stalls, and the food vendors cooking with cinnamon, cumin, coriander (cilantro), garlic, chillies, and the ubiquitous spice mix, zahtar.

Traditional foodstuffs

These are the everyday ingredients that play a huge role in the culinary world of the eastern Mediterranean, accompanying the abundant fresh vegetables, fruit and grains, the delicious meat and fish, and giving the region's food much of its characteristic flavour and texture.

Dairy products

Milk is rarely consumed on its own in Lebanon. Instead it is used to prepare butter, clarified butter, yogurt, cheese, and clotted cream, all of which are used every day. Some Bedouin use camel's milk and some peasants use the milk of water buffalo, but most milk comes from sheep, goats and cows. The milk, cheese and yogurt produced in the Bekaa Valley is regarded as superior to those produced everywhere else. The dairy foods of each region have their own special flavour and consistency, sometimes with the addition of herbs or garlic. In Lebanon, village women used to go from door to door carrying milk, cheese and yogurt on large trays balanced on their heads, but now there are dairy farms and most of the produce is transported to the towns by truck and sold in the markets.

Yogurt has formed an important part of the basic diet in the region since ancient times. Easily digestible and nutritious, it is served with rice and lentil dishes, or combined with other ingredients such as herbs, garlic and pulped vegetables to form a dip or salad. It is also mixed with water and a little salt to produce the regional drink called laban. Yogurt is thick and creamy, but for certain dishes it is strained through muslin (cheesecloth) to produce a dense cream-cheese consistency, which is ideal for mezze dishes. The thickest yogurt can also be moulded into balls for storing in olive oil.

Above: Most dairy products in Lebanon are made from the milk of goats or sheep.

Traditionally, butter was churned in the tanned skin of a whole goat. Partially filled with milk, and sealed at the ends, the skin was suspended by four ropes tied to the legs. The woman of the household would then sit beside the skin and jerk it to and fro until the milk was churned into butter – an age-old tradition that is still followed in remote villages and by the Bedouin in their temporary camps. Butter was used lavishly in medieval kitchens and still is by some Lebanese cooks, although olive oil and a variety of vegetable oils have largely replaced it. Hama, in Syria, has gained a reputation for its clarified butter, samna, which is used in some Lebanese dishes.

Laban

This refreshing yogurt drink is particularly popular among Muslims who drink it to quench their thirst or with a meal. Laban can be served plain or with dried mint or zahtar, or a dusting of cinnamon.

Serves 4–6

600ml/1 pint chilled thick, creamy yogurt

600ml/1 pint cold water

5ml/1 tsp dried mint

salt

In a jug (pitcher), whisk the yogurt with the water until foamy. Season to taste with salt. Drop several ice cubes into each glass and pour the yogurt mixture over the top. Sprinkle the surface with a little mint and serve immediately.

Olives

Olives and white cheese have provided sustenance for the peasants and nomads of the Fertile Crescent since ancient times, and custom has not changed this. In the mountain pastures of Lebanon or the fertile plains of Syria, the herders and travellers still munch on a few olives with a bit of cheese and perhaps some bread and dates to keep them going until the next meal. A Lebanese table would be incomplete without a bowl of locally harvested olives, which are often marinated in olive oil, thyme and lemon juice. The trees thrive on the stony hillsides of Lebanon and Syria, where they bear fruit for a long time, sometimes hundreds of years. There is an old Arab saying: 'In spite of hardship and neglect, the olive tree remains a strong and useful wife'.

A huge variety of olives are available in the markets, and certain villages are renowned for particular olives and the superb oil they produce. Collectively, Lebanon, Syria, Jordan and Turkey are the main producers of olive oil in the eastern Mediterranean and Middle East.

Above: Olive oil is used in every Lebanese meal, for cooking, dressing and enriching.

Bread

A meal without bread in Lebanon, Syria or Turkey is almost unthinkable. An essential component of every meal, leavened or unleavened bread is employed as a scoop, as a mop for soaking up the divine cooking juices on the plate, as a dipper to sink into a puréed, garlicky mezze dish, and as an all-round table accompaniment. Traditionally, bread was baked in the communal oven, the *furn*, or in a cylindrical oven made of clay, the *tanur*. In some rural areas, a small pit dug in the ground was used as the oven and flat breads were cooked over the fire on a *saaj*, a type of griddle. The communal baking at the village *furn* was a social occasion for the women, who gathered around the oven preparing the dough while they chatted and sang. All these methods of baking are still in use today, particularly in rural areas, but most urban neighbourhoods have a bakery.

Since medieval times, bread has been prepared with barley, millet and wheat, but corn was introduced during the Ottoman era and became a feature of many village loaves. The varied bread-making of the Ottoman Empire was remarked upon in the diaries and letters of travellers passing through Turkey and the Fertile Crescent. From the middle of the 17th century until the French occupation, Armenians monopolized the baking industry in Lebanon and Syria.

Below: A terraced olive grove near Moukhtara, in southern Lebanon.

Below: A light meal in Lebanon consists of a hunk of white cheese, olives and bread.

Above: Huge rounds of bread like this are cooked on special domed griddles.

Preserving

Curing and drying food is very important in the cultures of the eastern Mediterranean. Meat is preserved in its own fat; fleshy fruits, such as apricots, peaches, pears, cherries, mulberries and figs, are dried in the sun, as are bell peppers, aubergines (eggplants), okra and broad (fava) beans. Sour pomegranates and grapes are boiled down to syrupy molasses. Brine is used to preserve vine leaves and olives, which are also crushed to make oil, or preserved in salt. Tomatoes and bell peppers are reduced to pastes; yogurt is drained to make cheese and preserved in oil; and butter is clarified to keep for months. When plentiful, fish is dried and salted, or pickled, seasonal wild herbs are tied in bunches and hung up to dry, and roses and orange blossom are distilled to make flavoured waters. These

traditional seasonal activities are still part of daily life in many homes, but such foods are also commercially available.

Qawarma, a kind of preserved meat, is a traditional delicacy in Arab and Anatolian cooking, consisting of meat, generally lamb, preserved in its own fat. Following an ancient method, the meat is cut into small cubes and fried in its own fat, then stored in rendered fat in earthenware jars and reserved for flavouring eggs, soups and grains in the winter months, or when meat is scarce.

Pickles

In Lebanon, pickling is the most popular method of preserving food such as fruit, vegetables and nuts. The same methods are just as common in Syria, Jordan and Turkey, as the cooks of the whole region inherited their skills from the medieval Arabs, who were in turn influenced by the Greeks and Romans. The pickling of fruit and vegetables used to be vital to

Below: Truffles from Lebanon need careful cleaning to rid them of the desert sands.

Above: Lemons have been preserved for centuries, either in brine or packed in salt.

the diet, as there was a shortage of fresh produce in the winter and also in the arid desert areas. A wide variety of ingredients were pickled, often in colourful combinations.

Pickling is no longer so necessary, as fresh produce is available all year round, but it remains a popular tradition, partly because the results are so delicious and attractive. Favourite pickle combinations include pickled turnip with a few slices of beetroot (beet) to turn them a pretty shade of pink, or red cabbage with cauliflower, which produces a purple tint. Other pickles range from finely shredded cabbage together with apricots and green almonds to slices of aubergine (eggplant) wrapped around cloves of garlic and apricots and tied in a bundle with a thin ribbon of leek or celery.

Individual pickles include jars of green beans, white cabbage, the classic slim

Above: Tahini sauce is made from crushed sesame seeds and is used as a dressing.

green chilli peppers, okra, onions, little unripe tomatoes, green walnuts, almonds and beetroot (beets).

Vine leaves, garlic cloves, coriander seeds, cinnamon sticks, parsley stalks, allspice berries and thin, hot chillies are often added to the pickling jars, which are then filled to the brim with cider or white wine vinegar, sometimes diluted with water and often mixed with a little salt. The pickling liquor is as important as the pickled vegetable or fruit itself, as a thirst-quenching drink on a hot day.

Truffles

Although truffles are more commonly associated with the cuisines of France and Italy, they have been enjoyed in Lebanon and Syria for centuries. Some varieties of Lebanese truffle, kama, are found at the roots of particular trees on the hillsides, but the Syrian variety is

found in the desert. The most popular truffles, which are gathered and distributed throughout the eastern Mediterranean, grow in profusion around the oasis of Palmyra, situated on the ancient caravan route from Damascus to the Euphrates River. It is here that the Bedouin collect them and enjoy them boiled with buttermilk, or roasted in the ashes of the fire.

The black and white truffles of this region are mild in aroma and taste, and they are sold in the markets still covered in desert sand, which means they need very careful cleaning. Medieval recipes call for truffles to be boiled and dressed with oil and crushed thyme, or to be cooked with eggs or lamb. A traditional Lebanese method of preparing them is to cut them into cubes, which are then marinated and threaded on skewers to grill over a fire or barbecue.

Sesame seeds

These tiny, teardrop-shaped seeds seem almost indispensable in the Arab culinary world. They are sprinkled over a variety of savoury pastries and breads, added to salads, marinades and spice mixes such as zahtar, and crushed for their oil

Below: Sesame seeds are sprinkled over food, or crushed to make a creamy sauce.

and ground to a versatile creamy paste called tahini. This sesame paste can be found in light or dark varieties. The darker, coarser tahini is prepared from roasted sesame seeds and has a nuttier flavour than the lighter, creamier version.

In Lebanon tahini is a vital ingredient in the much-loved chickpea purée, hummus, and the national smoked aubergine mezze dish, baba ghanoush. Tahini is also often combined with lemon and crushed garlic to make a fragrant sauce for fish and vegetable dishes.

Pine nuts

In ancient times in the Fertile Crescent, pine nuts were included in the ceremonial offerings of fruit placed on statues that were erected to symbolize the wealth and status of towns and cities. The medieval Arabs added them liberally to savoury and sweet dishes, and the Ottomans used them in fillings for stuffed vegetables and leaves, and roasted them to sprinkle over desserts. With such a pine-nut heritage in their culinary background, the Lebanese could hardly ignore this pine cone seed, which has a mild resinous taste and is deliciously crunchy when roasted.

Below: Pine nuts are added to many Lebanese recipes, both savoury and sweet.

Spices, herbs and flavourings

With the Phoenician legacy of trading and the art of hospitality from the Arabs, it is not surprising that the stylish and vibrant cuisine of Lebanon is full of flavour and is often described as the 'pearl of the Arab kitchen'. Spices and herbs, nuts and seeds, and scented flavourings all play an important role in the cooking of the region. The following spices and flavourings are those you would find in a *munay*, the food cellar or larder of a Lebanese home.

Carob molasses

This is a thick, dark syrup obtained from the carob trees that grow well in the dry desert areas of Lebanon, Syria and Jordan. Originally, the syrup was used to sweeten drinks, desserts and stews. In Lebanon today there is a variety of syrups to choose from, such as date and grape mixtures, as well as carob. A sweet paste made with carob molasses and tahini is often served with bread for breakfast, but it can also be transformed into a savoury dish to be served as part of a mezze by spiking it with crushed garlic, lemon juice and dried mint.

Pomegranate syrup

Unlike carob molasses, this is sour. The syrup is much coveted for salad dressings and marinades and it is often drizzled over dishes for the exquisite fruity sour note it lends to them.

Below: Pomegranates

Sumac

This deep-red condiment is prepared by crushing and grinding the dried berries of a bush (*Rhus coriaria*) that grows wild in the mountains. The ground spice has a fruity sour taste and is often used as a substitute for lemons. It is also sprinkled over barbecued meats and fish.

Mastic

This is the aromatic gum from a small evergreen tree (*Pistacia lentiscus*) that grows wild all over the Mediterranean region. The distinctive flavour of mastic is employed to enhance milk puddings, jams, ice cream, and, sometimes, the aniseed-flavour spirit, arak.

Cinnamon

Brought to the region by Arab traders from Ceylon and the Spice Islands, cinnamon quickly became absorbed in the culinary culture of Lebanon. It is a pungent and warming spice, sold in stick or ground form and used in cakes, sweetmeats, meat stews and soups.

Cumin

These tiny seeds have a distinctive taste and, when roasted, they emit a delightful nutty aroma. Believed to aid digestion, cumin is used in a number of dishes that might cause a degree of indigestion or flatulence, such as bean dishes.

Coriander

The coriander (cilantro) plant has been cultivated in the eastern Mediterranean for medicinal and culinary purposes since ancient times. Sometimes referred to as 'Arab parsley', coriander leaves are fresh-smelling with a citrus taste. The seeds have a peppery flavour and, when roasted, emit a delicious nutty aroma.

Below: Cinnamon bark

Below: Spice mixes, zahtar and baharat

Above: Saffron strands

Above: Mint

Above: Rose petals

Saffron

Mainly cultivated in Turkey and neighbouring Iran, saffron consists of the orange stigmas of the purple crocus (*crocus sativus*). When soaked in water the stigmas impart a magnificent yellow dye and a hint of floral notes. It is used to add colour and flavour to the more sophisticated dishes of French-style restaurants and in festive feasts.

Garlic

Indigenous to the region, garlic has been used for both medicinal and culinary purposes since classical times. It was employed liberally in medieval Arab dishes, and has since become synonymous with Middle Eastern cooking. In the villages of Lebanon, Syria, Jordan and Turkey, whole heads of garlic are often threaded on to skewers with strips of fat from the sheep's tail and grilled over an open fire.

Flat leaf parsley

The leaves of this vigorous, strongly growing plant are probably the most popular fresh herb in the eastern Mediterranean, followed closely by mint and coriander (cilantro). Parsley is used in numerous dishes, and is also served on its own to sharpen the appetite, to cut the spice, to cleanse the palate, or to freshen the breath. The flat leaf variety of parsley has a very distinctive aroma and taste and there are many Middle Eastern dishes that just would not be the same without it. In Lebanon it is the principal feature of the national dish, tabbouleh, a parsley salad with bulgur wheat.

Mint

As mint grows prolifically throughout the eastern Mediterranean it finds its way into numerous salads, dips, soups such as shorbet khyar bi laban, based on chilled cucumber and yogurt, and some sweet dishes. With its refreshing and digestive qualities, fresh mint is one of the most useful herbs for cold dishes, whereas the dried herb is used in soups and stews. For medicinal purposes infusions made with the fresh or dried leaves are believed to relieve nausea, stomach disorders and sore throats.

Rose petals

The origins and uses of rose petals can be traced back to the ancient Egyptians, but the invention of distilled rose water for culinary purposes is attributed to the Persians. Adopted by the Arabs and later by the Ottomans, rose water has been used from the sumptuous medieval dishes of the banquets of Baghdad to the modern sophisticated puddings of Istanbul. In Lebanon, rose petals are used to garnish puddings, and rose water, along with orange flower water, is used to flavour syrups for a variety of desserts. It is also the main ingredient of the popular sherbet drink, sharab al ward, often served to welcome guests.

Spice mixes

Throughout the Middle East you will come across a spice mix called baharat. Generally this spice mix includes black pepper, coriander seeds, cumin, cinnamon, cardamom, cloves, nutmeg and paprika but, in Lebanon, it is often referred to as sabaa baharat, which means it contains seven of these spices – cardamom would be the one to omit.

Zahtar is the Arabic word for thyme, which grows wild in the hills of Lebanon. It is also the word for the tasty spice mix which is sprinkled over bread, cheese, yogurt and salads and is a favourite seasoning for street vendors throughout Egypt and the Fertile Crescent as they add it liberally to beans, cooked meats, kibbeh, and other hot, savoury snacks. Consisting primarily of dried thyme, ground sumac and salt, it is fairly easy to prepare a batch at home.

Traditional drinks

Lebanon, Syria, Jordan and Turkey all share similar gestures of hospitality. For example, it is traditional to offer coffee or tea to a guest to welcome them into a home. Similarly, it is polite to accept the drink, otherwise you are seen to be rejecting a kind offer of hospitality.

Coffee

The introduction of coffee from Yemen into the eastern Mediterranean in the 15th and 16th centuries made a significant impact on the social life of the region, as it heralded the institution of the coffee house, a strictly male domain. The drinking of coffee thus became primarily a male pastime, although women who could afford it enjoyed coffee in their own homes. The Ottoman Turks adopted the coffee house and introduced it to Istanbul, where the institution still survives, rivalling the best in Beirut, Damascus and Aleppo.

Some of the coffee houses were extremely fine and luxurious establishments, private meeting places for the noble and rich; others were less sophisticated but no less pleasing, as the locations were selected for their small scented gardens or shady trees, such as the famous coffee houses along the tree-lined banks of the River Barada. In the evenings some coffee houses provided entertainment: professional dancers, singers, musicians and storytellers. In Lebanon, particularly in Beirut, there are also a number of modern French-style cafés which, unlike some of the traditional coffee houses, are open to people of all ages, women as well as men.

Generally, two styles of coffee are on offer in the region: Turkish and Arabic. Turkish coffee is very finely ground and brewed in a small, long-handled pot called a *rakwi* in Arabic and a *cezve* in Turkish; the result is thick and grainy, and is sweetened according to taste – sweet (*hilweh*), medium sweet (*wassat*) or without sugar (*murra*) – while it is bubbling up to form a froth on top. Arabic coffee, on the other hand, is generally prepared in two pots, called *dallahs*. The first is used for making the brew of ground coffee beans and boiling water, which is then poured into the second pot leaving the grains behind. Cloves, cardamom pods, cinnamon sticks and orange flower or rose water are often added to enhance the flavour of Arabic coffee. It is the custom to serve a glass of water with the thick coffee and in some areas only one cup of coffee will be offered. Among the Bedouin, however, coffee flows like the wine of ancient Rome: when your cup is empty it will always be filled up, as the Bedouin thrive on their strong coffee, which they grind by hand and drink black and bitter.

The reading of fortunes from the sediment left at the bottom of the coffee cup is a popular pastime throughout the region. First the cups are inverted on to the saucers to allow the grains to drip downward, forming patterns on the inside of the cup. Readings are then made from the lines and patterns on the cup, followed by the saucer, which is held above the cup to catch the drips.

Tea

Surrounded by less ritual and fewer customs, tea holds its own significance in the culinary and social culture of the

Left: Small cups of thick coffee are enjoyed at the end of a large meal.

region. Generally, it is made strong and is sweetened with sugar, either by stirring it into the hot liquid, or by holding a sugar lump between the teeth and sipping the tea through it. Sometimes herbs and spices, such as mint or aniseed, are added to the tea in Jordan and Lebanon.

Numerous herb- and floral-based teas are also enjoyed, such as thyme, lemon verbena, jasmine and camomile. Some types of herb tea are brewed for colds, or to aid the digestion; others are thought to increase fertility.

Wine

Although winemaking took place in Greater Syria, and the ancient Egyptians, Phoenicians and Romans all enjoyed wine, its consumption was curtailed by the introduction of Islam. Arabs had drunk wine and the local spirit, arak, before the Islamic revolution, and Lebanon was regarded as one of the prime producers, but excessive drunkenness and gambling led to its prohibition. However, the Christian and Jewish communities continued to make wine, exporting it to Europe from Tyre

Below: As in most Middle Eastern countries, Lebanese tea is served without milk and with plenty of sugar.

and Sidon. Not all Muslims were strict converts to the new prohibitions and the most notorious offenders were often the noblemen, caliphs and judges.

Wine was also produced in Ottoman Syria, particularly by the monasteries, and the Rothschild family produced wine near Jaffa in Palestine from the 1880s. The quality of Lebanese wine, however, continued to surpass that of its neighbours: one white wine, produced near Beirut, was described as the champagne of the east. Other high-quality wines were produced in the Armenian Catholic monastery of Bzummar, the Maronite monastery of Cannobin, and the town of Zahleh. Naturally, when the French occupied Lebanon they produced their own wines in Aleppo, Beirut, Baalbek and Shtora.

Lebanon's wines are still admired to this day, and some of its vines are reputed to date back to the Crusades. The fertile soil of the Bekaa Valley produces excellent grapes. With such ancient vines interspersed with more recent French and American varieties, the resulting vintages are interestingly complex and are celebrated every year

Above: The lush area of the Bekaa Valley is where most of Lebanon's vines grow, producing a wide variety of grapes.

at the wine festival held in Zahleh. a town devoted to wine production, a fact underlined by the large statue of Bacchus you see as you enter it.

Beer and spirits

Other alcoholic beverages of Lebanon, Jordan and Syria include beer and arak, a clear spirit distilled from grapes and flavoured with aniseed, which turns cloudy when water is added, just like the raki of Turkey and the ouzo of Greece. Although beer is mentioned in some early records, it was really only during the post-Ottoman period that it was mass-produced, each region boasting its own light, refreshing brew. The enjoyment of arak, on the other hand, has been well documented and remains hugely popular as the drink to accompany mezze – it could be said, in some cases, that the mezze is a necessary accompaniment to the arak! Once again Zahleh is famous for its arak, which enhances the town's reputation as a food lover's paradise.

MEZZE & SALADS

Olive and pepper salad

Fried halloumi with zahtar

Parsley salad with bulgur

Smoked aubergine dip

Lebanese chickpea dip

Toasted bread salad with sumac

Bean salad with garlic and coriander

Chicken wings with garlic and sumac

Lebanese country salad

Smoked aubergine with walnuts and pomegranate seeds

Chickpea and bulgur salad with mint

Cheese and yogurt dip with zahtar

A tantalizing array of little dishes

The tradition of mezze is one of the most enjoyable features of the culinary culture of the eastern Mediterranean, and without doubt, mezze dishes (also called mazza in Lebanon) can be the best part of a Lebanese meal. The pursuit of leisure is ingrained in the region's social life, whether it is playing backgammon in a teahouse, smoking a hubble-bubble in a coffee-house or relaxing in a steam bath. All these activities can be accompanied by a little light refreshment: eating is the ultimate form of leisure here. Nothing quite beats mezze in the shade of an old fig tree, on a balcony overlooking cobbled streets, at a sea-front table, or indoors seated around a low table set with a tempting selection of dishes.

The concept of mezze is an old one. The word is thought to derive from the Persian *maza*, meaning 'taste' or 'relish', or from the Arabic verb, *mazmiz*, 'to nibble at food'. In Lebanon both wine and arak are crucial to the enjoyment of mezze. Snacks and appetizers that are served with non-alcoholic drinks, such as tea or a sherbet drink, are generally referred to as muqabbalat rather than mezze.

Everyone helps themselves to an assortment of little dishes, which can range from olives, nuts, dips and salads to hot pastries, meatballs, kibbeh, stuffed vegetables, grilled shellfish and Arab pizzas. Salads can range from a bowl of vegetables to dishes prepared with eggs, beans, truffles, fish and lambs' brains. Delightful to look at and often surprising to the palate, mezze is a wonderful way to eat and can form an entire meal. However, when sharing mezze with Lebanese, it is easy to forget that it is often only a prelude to the ensuing meat, rice and vegetable dishes, so a degree of restraint is required.

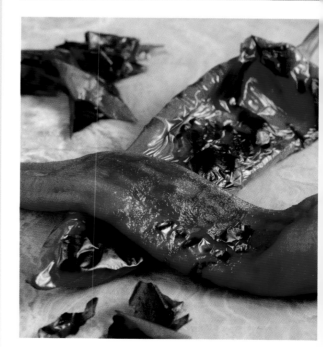

Serves 4–6

2 long, red Mediterranean peppers, or red or orange (bell) peppers

30–45ml/2–3 tbsp Kalamata or other fleshy black olives

30–45ml/2–3 tbsp fleshy green olives

1 large tomato, skinned, seeded and diced

2 spring onions (scallions), trimmed and finely sliced

30ml/2 tbsp olive oil

juice of 1 lemon

small handful of fresh mint leaves, roughly chopped

small bunch of fresh coriander (cilantro), roughly chopped

sea salt and ground black pepper

Olive and pepper salad
Salatet zaytoon

Almost every hillside in the eastern Mediterranean is dotted with olive trees, and most villages have a communal olive press where the harvest can be crushed for its valuable, fruity oil. Olives appear on most mezze tables, marinated in oil and herbs or spices, or tossed in a refreshing salad.

1 Place the peppers on a hot griddle, or directly over a gas flame or charcoal grill, turning until the skin is evenly charred. Leave them in a plastic bag for a few minutes to sweat, then hold each one under cold running water and peel off the skin. Remove the stalks and seeds, dice the flesh and place in a bowl.

2 Pit the olives and slice them in half lengthways. Add the halves to the bowl with the chopped peppers.

3 Add the tomatoes, spring onions and herbs and pour in the oil and lemon juice. Season and toss well. Serve with warm pitta bread as part of a mezze spread.

Energy 68kcal/283kJ; Protein 1.1g; Carbohydrate 4.6g, of which sugars 4.4g; Fat 5.2g, of which saturates 0.8g; Cholesterol 0mg; Calcium 30mg; Fibre 1.9g; Sodium 232mg

Fried halloumi with zahtar
Hallum

Available in Arab markets and most supermarkets, halloumi is a salty, firm white cheese. In Lebanon, it is made from cow's milk and matured in whey, sometimes combined with nigella seeds, mint or thyme. Generally, it is used in savoury pastries, or slices are grilled or fried and served as a mezze dish. Serve it straight from the pan, as it becomes rubbery when cool.

1 Rinse the halloumi under cold running water and pat dry with kitchen paper. Using a sharp knife, cut into thin slices.

2 Heat the oil in a heavy-based pan. Fry the halloumi slices for 2 minutes until golden, then flip over and fry the other side. Drain on kitchen paper.

3 Transfer the hot halloumi on to a serving dish and sprinkle with zahtar. Eat immediately, with some Lebanese flat bread and a squeeze of lemon.

Energy 328kcal/1356kJ; Protein 16.2g; Carbohydrate 1.7g, of which sugars 0g; Fat 28.6g, of which saturates 13.1g; Cholesterol 48mg; Calcium 311mg; Fibre 0g; Sodium 331mg

Serves 2–4

45–60ml/3–4 tbsp olive oil

250g/9oz plain halloumi cheese

15ml/1 tbsp zahtar

lemon wedges and Lebanese flat bread, to accompany

Parsley salad with bulgur
Tabbouleh

The main ingredient of this classic Lebanese salad is parsley, flavoured with a hint of mint and tossed with a little fine bulgur so that the grains resemble tiny gems in a sea of green. The key to its preparation is to slice the parsley finely, rather than chop it, so that the strands remain dry and fresh, not mushy. Tabbouleh is also a refreshing accompaniment to grilled meats.

1 Rinse the bulgur in cold water and drain well. Place it in a bowl and pour over the lemon juice. Leave to soften for 10 minutes while you prepare the salad.

2 With the parsley tightly bunched, slice the leaves as finely as you can with a sharp knife. Transfer the parsley into a bowl. Slice the mint leaves and add them to the bowl with the tomatoes, spring onions and the soaked bulgur. Pour in the oil, season with salt and pepper and toss the salad gently.

3 Serve immediately, so that the herbs do not get the chance to soften. Arrange the lettuce leaves around the salad and use them to scoop up the tabbouleh.

Energy 232kcal/965kJ; Protein 5.2g; Carbohydrate 34.6g, of which sugars 2.7g; Fat 8.4g, of which saturates 1.1g; Cholesterol 0mg; Calcium 51mg; Fibre 1.4g; Sodium 12mg

Serves 4–6

65g/2¹/₂oz/¹/₂ cup fine bulgur

juice of 2 lemons

large bunch of flat leaf parsley (about 225g/8oz)

handful of fresh mint leaves

2–3 tomatoes, skinned, seeded and finely diced

4 spring onions (scallions), trimmed and finely sliced

60ml/4 tbsp olive oil

sea salt and ground black pepper

1 cos or romaine lettuce, trimmed and split into leaves, to serve

Serves 4–6

2 large aubergines (eggplants)

30–45ml/2–3 tbsp tahini

juice of 1–2 lemons

30–45ml/2–3 tbsp strained yogurt

2 cloves garlic, crushed

small bunch of flat leaf parsley, finely chopped

sea salt and ground black pepper

olive oil, for drizzling

Cook's tip If grilled over charcoal the aubergine (eggplant) skin toughens, and it is easier to slit it open and scoop out the softened flesh.

Smoked aubergine dip
Baba ghanoush

There are variations of this classic dish, also known as moutabal. Some cooks add chopped flat leaf parsley or coriander (cilantro) while others lighten it with a little yogurt or lemon juice. The dish has a strong smoky flavour, which is best enjoyed with crusty bread, or pitta, to dip into it.

1 Place the aubergines on a hot griddle, or directly over a gas flame or charcoal grill, turning them from time to time, until they are soft to touch and the skin is charred and flaky. Place them in a plastic bag for a few minutes to sweat and, when cool enough to handle, hold them by the stems under cold running water and peel off the skin. Squeeze out the excess water and chop the flesh to a pulp.

2 Beat the tahini with the lemon juice – the mixture stiffens at first, then loosens to a creamy paste. Beat in the yogurt and then, using a fork, beat in the aubergine pulp.

3 Add the garlic and parsley (reserving a little to garnish), season well with salt and pepper and beat the mixture thoroughly. Turn the mixture into a serving dish, drizzle a little olive oil over the top to keep it moist and sprinkle with the reserved parsley.

Energy 91kcal/375kJ; Protein 1g; Carbohydrate 2.2g, of which sugars 1.5g; Fat 8.8g, of which saturates 1.4g; Cholesterol 8mg; Calcium 8mg; Fibre 1.4g; Sodium 52mg

Serves 4–6

225g/8oz dried chickpeas, soaked in water for at least 6 hours, or overnight

45–60ml/3–4 tbsp olive oil

1–2 cloves garlic, crushed

juice of 1 lemon

juice of 1 Seville orange, or ½ large orange

45–60ml/3–4 tbsp tahini

sea salt and freshly ground black pepper

pitta bread or crudités, to serve

To garnish

15ml/1 tbsp olive oil

small bunch of fresh coriander (cilantro), finely chopped

Lebanese chickpea dip
Hummus bil tahina

This classic dip can, of course, be bought ready-made, but made at home it can be varied widely to taste – some enjoy it spiked with cumin, garlic or chilli; others prefer it light and lemony. There are dense versions thickened with tahini and refreshing versions flavoured with orange juice or fresh herbs.

1 Drain the chickpeas and place them in a pan with plenty of water. Bring to the boil, reduce the heat and simmer, covered, for about 1½ hours, until the chickpeas are very soft. Drain, reserving a few spoonfuls of the cooking liquid, and remove any loose skins. Put the chickpeas and liquid into a blender or food processor.

2 Whizz the chickpeas to a thick purée. Add the olive oil, garlic, lemon and orange juices and tahini and blend thoroughly. Season with salt and pepper to taste.

3 Turn the hummus into a serving bowl and drizzle a little oil over the surface to keep it moist. Sprinkle with a little coriander and serve with strips of warm pitta bread or crudités such as carrot, celery and (bell) pepper sticks.

Energy 265kcal/1101kJ; Protein 10g; Carbohydrate 12.6g, of which sugars 0.8g; Fat 19.7g, of which saturates 2.8g; Cholesterol 0mg; Calcium 210mg; Fibre 4.7g; Sodium 15mg

Toasted bread salad with sumac
Fattoush

This is one of the classic Lebanese dishes that were devised to make use of leftover bread. Sumac, the deep red, fruity spice ground from the berries of a bush native to the eastern Mediterranean, is an essential component.

1 First, prepare the flat bread. Toast it briefly on both sides, then break it into bitesize pieces. Set aside.

2 Trim and chop the lettuce leaves, seed and chop the skinned tomatoes, peel and slice the carrot, trim and slice the radishes, seed and chop the peppers, and trim and slice the spring onions. Place all the vegetables in a bowl.

3 In a jar or a small bowl, whisk the olive oil with the lemon juice and garlic to make the dressing.

4 Add the chopped parsley to the vegetables, together with the pieces of bread, then pour the dressing over the salad. Sprinkle the sumac over the top and season with salt and pepper. Toss the salad well, making sure the bread is well coated in the oil and sumac. Serve immediately as part of a mezze spread, or on its own as a snack or light lunch.

Energy 120kcal/499kJ; Protein 2.4g; Carbohydrate 7.7g, of which sugars 7.5g; Fat 9.1g, of which saturates 1.4g; Cholesterol 0mg; Calcium 54mg; Fibre 3g; Sodium 18mg

Serves 4–6

1–2 flat breads, such as pitta breads

$1/2$ cos or romaine lettuce,

2–3 tomatoes, skinned

1 carrot

5–6 small radishes

1 red or green (bell) pepper

4–5 spring onions (scallions)

small bunch of flat leaf parsley

60–75ml/4–5 tbsp olive oil

juice of 1 lemon

1–2 cloves garlic, crushed

10–15ml/2–3 tsp ground sumac

sea salt and ground black pepper

Bean salad with garlic and coriander
Foul moukala

This traditional salad is popular as a mezze dish but it is also served as an accompaniment to grilled meats. It is always made when fresh broad beans are in season but it is also very good when prepared with frozen beans.

1 Put the shelled beans in a pan with just enough water to cover. Stir in the sugar to preserve the colour of the beans, and bring the water to the boil. Reduce the heat and simmer, uncovered, for about 15 minutes, until the beans are cooked but remain al dente.

2 Drain the beans and refresh them under running cold water, then drain again and put them in a bowl.

3 Toss the beans in the oil, lemon juice and garlic. Season well with salt and pepper to taste, and stir in the coriander.

Energy 111kcal/464kJ; Protein 6.8g; Carbohydrate 10.7g, of which sugars 2g; Fat 4.8g, of which saturates 0.7g; Cholesterol 0mg; Calcium 64mg; Fibre 5.8g; Sodium 10mg

Serves 4–6

500g/1¹/₄lb/3¹/₂ cups shelled broad (fava) beans

5ml/1 tsp sugar

30–45ml/2–3 tbsp olive oil

juice of ¹/₂ lemon

1–2 cloves garlic, crushed

sea salt and ground black pepper

small bunch of fresh coriander (cilantro), finely chopped

Cook's tip If you prefer to serve the salad cold it can be prepared in advance, but it is also good eaten while the beans are still warm. In this case simply drain them without refreshing under cold water, toss them in the oil then add the other ingredients and serve immediately.

Serves 4–6

45–60ml/3–4 tbsp olive oil

juice of 1 lemon

4 cloves garlic, crushed

15ml/1 tbsp ground sumac

16–20 chicken wings

sea salt

Chicken wings with garlic and sumac
Jawaneh

The aroma of chicken wings or drumsticks grilling over charcoal is always enticing, whether it is in a busy street market or in a clearing in the countryside. Great street and picnic food, these tasty chicken wings are best eaten with your fingers, straight from the oven, grill or barbecue.

1 In a bowl, mix together the olive oil, lemon juice, garlic and sumac. Place the chicken wings in a shallow dish and rub the marinade all over them. Cover the dish and leave to marinate in the refrigerator for 2 hours.

2 Prepare the barbecue or preheat a conventional grill (broiler). Place the chicken wings on the rack and cook for about 3 minutes on each side, basting them with the marinade while they cook. Alternatively, preheat the oven to 180°C/350°F/ Gas 4, place the chicken wings in an ovenproof dish, brush with the marinade and roast for 25–30 minutes.

3 When the wings are completely cooked, remove from the heat, sprinkle with salt and serve while still hot.

Energy 272kcal/1132kJ; Protein 23g; Carbohydrate 1.4g, of which sugars 0.1g; Fat 19.5g, of which saturates 4.7g; Cholesterol 98mg; Calcium 12mg; Fibre 0.1g; Sodium 68mg

Serves 4–6

| |
1 cos or romaine lettuce

1 cucumber

2 tomatoes

2–3 spring onions (scallions)

bunch of fresh mint leaves

bunch of flat leaf parsley

30ml/2 tbsp olive oil

juice of $\frac{1}{2}$ lemon

sea salt

Lebanese country salad
Salatah Lebanieh

Each region of the eastern Mediterranean has its own version of a classic salad, which is often described as originating with shepherds, gypsies, travellers or, in some cases, monks or priests. This is a typical, everyday, country salad that can be served as an accompaniment to any Lebanese dish, as well as part of a mezze spread.

1 Cut the lettuce leaves into bitesize chunks and place in a bowl. Partially peel the cucumber and cut into small chunks, skin the tomatoes and dice the flesh, trim and slice the spring onions and add all the vegetables to the bowl.

2 Wash and finely chop the mint and parsley, discarding the stalks, and add to the vegetables. Toss in the olive oil and lemon juice. Sprinkle with salt and serve.

Energy 51kcal/210kJ; Protein 1.1g; Carbohydrate 2.5g, of which sugars 2.4g; Fat 4.1g, of which saturates 0.6g; Cholesterol 0mg; Calcium 36mg; Fibre 1.3g; Sodium 8mg

Smoked aubergine with walnuts and pomegranate seeds
Batinjan rahib

Variations of this excellent salad can be found throughout the eastern Mediterranean. Serve it either warm or at room temperature to make the most of the subtle, smoky flavour of the aubergine.

1 Place the aubergines on a hot ridged griddle, or directly over a gas flame or a charcoal grill, and leave to char until soft, turning them from time to time. Hold the aubergines by their stems under running cold water and peel off the charred skins, or slit open the skins and scoop out the flesh.

2 Squeeze out the excess water from the aubergine flesh then chop it to a pulp and place it in a bowl with the tomatoes, pepper, onion, parsley and garlic. Add the olive oil and lemon juice and toss thoroughly. Season to taste with salt and pepper, then stir in half the walnuts and pomegranate seeds.

3 Turn the salad into a serving dish and garnish with the remaining walnuts and pomegranate seeds.

Energy 90kcal/374kJ; Protein 2.2g; Carbohydrate 7.3g, of which sugars 6.3g; Fat 6g, of which saturates 0.8g; Cholesterol 0mg; Calcium 39mg; Fibre 3.1g; Sodium 10mg

Serves 4–6

2 aubergines (eggplants)

2 tomatoes, skinned, seeded and chopped

1 green (bell) pepper, chopped

1 red onion, finely chopped

bunch of flat leaf parsley, finely chopped

2 cloves garlic, crushed

30–45ml/2–3 tbsp olive oil

juice of 1 lemon

15–30ml/1–2 tbsp walnuts, finely chopped

15–30ml/1–2 tbsp pomegranate seeds

sea salt and ground black pepper

Chickpea and bulgur salad with mint
Safsouf

This is a traditional village salad, using vegetarian ingredients that are readily available in the hills and valleys of Lebanon. The mixture can also be used as a filling for stuffed vine leaves or peppers and aubergines when meat is scarce. To prepare it as a salad, the ingredients are simply bound with olive oil and lemon juice and tossed with lots of fresh mint.

1 Place the bulgur in a bowl and pour over boiling water to cover. Leave to soak for 10–15 minutes, until it has doubled in volume.

2 Meanwhile, place the chickpeas in a bowl with the onion, sesame seeds and garlic and bind with the olive oil and lemon juice.

3 Squeeze the bulgur to remove any excess water and add it to the chickpeas with the parsley and mint. Toss well, season with salt and pepper to taste, and sprinkle the paprika over the top.

Energy 267kcal/1116kJ; Protein 8.6g; Carbohydrate 34.1g, of which sugars 3.3g; Fat 11.4g, of which saturates 1.4g; Cholesterol 0mg; Calcium 89mg; Fibre 4.1g; Sodium 153mg

Serves 4–6

150g/5oz/scant 1 cup fine bulgur, rinsed

400g/14oz canned chickpeas, drained and rinsed

1 red onion, finely chopped

15–30ml/1–2 tbsp toasted sesame seeds

2–3 cloves garlic, crushed

60–75ml/4–5 tbsp olive oil

juice of 1–2 lemons

bunch of flatleaf parsley, finely chopped

large bunch of mint, coarsely chopped

sea salt and ground black pepper

5ml/1 tsp paprika, to garnish

Cook's tip To toast sesame seeds, heat a frying pan, pour in enough seeds to just cover the bottom of the pan, then dry-fry over a low heat, stirring constantly, until the seeds turn golden brown. Remove from the pan immediately, and leave to cool. Alternatively, spread the sesame seeds on a baking tray and roast in a medium oven for a few minutes until golden brown. You need to keep a close eye on the seeds with either method, as they burn quickly.

Serves 6

250g/9oz feta cheese

250g/9oz/generous 1 cup thick, strained yogurt

30ml/2 tbsp olive oil

15ml/1 tbsp zahtar

Cook's tip You can buy strained yogurt to make this dish, or strain it yourself by draining it through muslin (cheesecloth) in a colander. The longer it is left the thicker it becomes. In Lebanon, labneh is eaten spread on bread with herbs or olives, or rolled into solid balls and steeped in olive oil.

Cheese and yogurt dip with zahtar
Jibne wa labneh

Cheese and yogurt are made in the villages of Lebanon from the milk of goats, ewes, or cows. Labneh is thick, creamy yogurt obtained by draining the everyday set yogurt through muslin. This combination of village cheese and labneh is creamy and slightly sour. Sprinkled with thyme or zahtar, it is popular as a dip for crudités or toasted flat bread.

1 Drain and rinse the feta cheese and pat dry with kitchen paper. Place the feta in a bowl and mash it with a fork.

2 Beat the strained yogurt into the feta to form a thick paste. Spread the mixture in a shallow dish and drizzle the olive oil over the top.

3 Sprinkle with the zahtar before serving.

Energy 192kcal/797kJ; Protein 9.5g; Carbohydrate 2.3g, of which sugars 1.5g; Fat 16.7g, of which saturates 8.4g; Cholesterol 29mg; Calcium 217mg; Fibre 0g; Sodium 631mg

SOUPS, BREADS & HOT SNACKS

Chicken and saffron broth
with noodles

Lamb and wheat soup

Creamy red lentil soup
with cumin

Cucumber and yogurt soup

Pitta bread

Little flat breads with thyme
and sumac

Bulgur and lamb patties

Spicy bean balls

Lebanese meat pastries

Cheese and dill pastries

Spinach pastries with pine nuts

Cheese omelette with peppers
and olives

Warming soups and tasty snacks

Lebanese soups are hearty and satisfying, as they are often eaten first thing in the morning or last thing at night, and are also enjoyed as warming snacks at any time of day, particularly in chilly mountain air. The most famous is hreesi (harissa), traditionally made when the annual supply of qawarma – meat preserved in fat – was prepared. The meat is slow-cooked with its own fat and beaten until it resembles porridge, hence its name, which means 'mashed' or 'puréed' in Arabic.

Many street vendors sell a variety of soups as well as hot snacks prepared from bread and pastry dough. Lebanon boasts a huge variety of savoury pastries, many of which were introduced by the Ottoman Turks. Bread dough is used to make tasty snacks such as the famous manakakeish bil zahtar, little flat breads smeared with a paste made from thyme and sumac. A favourite street snack, loved by children, is kahk, sesame-covered bread shaped like a thick bracelet. The commonest bread is khubz arabi, or simply khubz, a round, flat, slightly leavened loaf of differing sizes, sometimes with a hollow pouch that can be filled for a tasty snack.

Bread is regarded as a gift from God: it should only be broken by hand, as to cut it with a knife would be like raising a sword against God. If a piece accidentally falls to the ground, it is picked up and symbolically pressed to the lips and forehead as a mark of respect. Leftover bread is never thrown away, but used in a number of sweet and savoury dishes. Throughout the region, bread is an essential part of every meal. In cities most people buy it still warm from their neighbourhood baker, sometimes two or three times a day, so that each meal is graced with a fresh loaf.

Chicken and saffron broth with noodles
Shorbet al dajaj

The more delicate Lebanese soups are generally served as an appetizer to a meal, whereas hearty soups made with vegetables and lentils, or meat and grain, may be served as a meal or snack on their own. This soup falls into another camp, as the cleansing broth with its floral notes of saffron is sometimes served as a palate cleanser between courses.

1 To make the stock, place all the chopped vegetables in a large pan. Put the chicken on top of the vegetables, and add the parsley, peppercorns and allspice berries. Pour in just enough water to cover the chicken.

2 Bring the water to the boil, then reduce the heat, cover the pan and simmer gently for about 1¹/₂ hours, until the chicken is practically falling off the bones.

3 Lift the chicken out of the pan and set aside. Strain the stock into a fresh pan and discard the vegetables and spices.

4 When the chicken is cool enough to handle, pull the meat off the carcass. Discard the bones and reserve the dark meat for another dish. Use your fingers to tear the breast meat into thin strips, cover and keep warm.

5 Reheat the broth and stir in the saffron fronds. Bring the broth to the boil and add the noodles. Reduce the heat and boil gently for about 10 minutes until the noodles are cooked.

6 Add the chicken strips to the soup and heat through. Check the seasoning and add salt and pepper to taste. Pour the hot soup into individual bowls and sprinkle with a little parsley or mint before serving.

Serves 6–8

For the stock

2 celery stalks, with leaves, roughly chopped

2 carrots, peeled and roughly chopped

1 onion, roughly chopped

1 lean, organic chicken, about 1.5kg/3¹/₄lb, cleaned and trimmed

small bunch of parsley, roughly chopped

6 peppercorns

6 allspice berries

For the broth

generous pinch of saffron fronds

115g/4oz/1 cup vermicelli, or other noodles, broken into pieces

sea salt and ground black pepper

small bunch of fresh parsley or mint, finely chopped, to garnish

Cook's tip Chicken stock will remain clear if the water is simmered gently rather than boiled, but if it does become cloudy don't worry, the flavour is not impaired, and some say that the stock becomes more nutritious if it is boiled rather than simmered.

Energy 260kcal/1088kJ; Protein 28.4g; Carbohydrate 11.3g, of which sugars 0g; Fat 11.3g, of which saturates 3.4g; Cholesterol 86mg; Calcium 17mg; Fibre 0g; Sodium 106mg

Lamb and wheat soup
Hreesi

This traditional peasant soup is prepared with lamb or chicken, combined with wheat and cooked slowly until it is the consistency of porridge. It makes a substantial meal. In Lebanon, the Christian communities often prepare this dish for the Feast of the Assumption, while Muslims traditionally eat it to break their fast at Ramadan. In some regions of the eastern Mediterranean the soup is prepared for wedding feasts.

1 Place the lamb in a large pan and pour in enough water to cover the meat. Bring the water to the boil and skim off any foam.

2 Drain the wheat and add it to the pan. Season with salt and lots of pepper, reduce the heat, cover and simmer for 1½–2 hours, until the meat is tender and the wheat is soft – top up with a little extra water, if necessary, during cooking.

3 Lift out the lamb shanks and remove the meat from the bones. Shred the meat into fine strands, using your fingers or two forks, and return it to the pan.

4 Continue to simmer the meat with the wheat, beating the mixture with a wooden spoon until it has the consistency of thick porridge. Adjust the seasoning, if necessary, turn off the heat, and cover with a lid to keep warm.

5 Heat a small frying pan and dry fry the cumin seeds until they begin to release their fragrance – be careful not to let them scorch. Add the ghee or butter and allow it to melt, then stir in the cinnamon.

6 Ladle the steaming hreesi into warmed bowls and press the back of a spoon into the middle of each bowlful to make a hollow. Pour some of the spiced melted butter into each hollow and serve immediately.

Energy 364kcal/1516kJ; Protein 18.8g; Carbohydrate 29.2g, of which sugars 0g; Fat 19.4g, of which saturates 9.8g; Cholesterol 73mg; Calcium 25mg; Fibre 0g; Sodium 73mg

Above: Standing and fallen columns at the temple to Bacchus in Baalbek.

Serves 4–6

900g/2lb lamb shanks

225g/8oz/1¼ cups wholegrain wheat, soaked in water overnight

10ml/2 tsp cumin seeds

30–45ml/2–3 tbsp ghee or butter

10ml/2 tsp ground cinnamon

sea salt and ground black pepper

Serves 4

225g/8oz/1 cup red lentils

30ml/2 tbsp olive oil

40g/1¹/₂oz butter

10ml/2 tsp cumin seeds

2 onions, chopped

1 litre/1³/₄ pints/4 cups chicken stock

5–10ml/1–2 tsp ground cumin

sea salt and ground black pepper

1 lemon, cut into wedges, to serve

60ml/4 tbsp strained yogurt, to serve (optional)

Creamy red lentil soup with cumin
Crema shorba al-adas

Lentil and grain soups, often containing chunks of meat or vegetables, are common fare throughout the Middle East, but every so often you come across a simple, puréed soup, flavoured with a single ingredient such as mint or cumin, which is very pleasantly refreshing.

1 Rinse the lentils and leave to drain. Heat the oil and butter in a large, heavy pan and stir in the cumin seeds. Cook, stirring, until they emit a nutty aroma. Add the onion, and when it begins to turn golden brown stir in the lentils.

2 Pour the stock into the pan and bring to the boil. Reduce the heat, cover the pan and simmer for about 30 minutes, topping up with water if necessary. Ladle the mixture into a food processor or blender and whizz to a smooth purée.

3 Return the soup to the pan to reheat, season with salt and pepper and ladle it into individual bowls. Dust with a little ground cumin and serve with lemon wedges to squeeze over. Add a spoonful of yogurt to each bowl, if you like.

Energy 235kcal/991kJ; Protein 13g; Carbohydrate 28.4g, of which sugars 3.7g; Fat 8.9g, of which saturates 2.2g; Cholesterol 0mg; Calcium 66mg; Fibre 2.9g; Sodium 40mg

Cucumber and yogurt soup
Shorbet khyar bi laban

In Turkey and Syria, a popular dish of cucumber combined with yogurt and mint is served as an accompaniment, whereas the Lebanese enjoy a similar combination in a cold soup. Middle Eastern cooks believe that salting the cucumber before using in salads and soups makes it easier to digest.

1 Place the cucumber slices on a plate and sprinkle them with salt. Leave to weep for 10–15 minutes, then gather the cucumber slices in your hands and squeeze gently to remove the salt and excess water. Meanwhile, chop the mint, reserving a few leaves for garnishing.

2 In a bowl, beat the yogurt with the garlic and mint. Stir in the water to thin it down and fold in the cucumber. Adjust the seasoning, cover and chill for 1–2 hours.

3 When ready to serve, place 2 or 3 ice cubes in each bowl and ladle the chilled soup over them. Garnish with the reserved mint leaves.

Energy 77kcal/322kJ; Protein 6.9g; Carbohydrate 10.3g, of which sugars 10.1g; Fat 1.3g, of which saturates 0.6g; Cholesterol 2mg; Calcium 255mg; Fibre 0.3g; Sodium 106mg

Serves 4

1 large cucumber, peeled, quartered lengthways and finely sliced

handful of fresh mint leaves

600ml/1 pint/2½ cups thick, creamy yogurt

2 cloves garlic, crushed

300ml/½ pint/1¼ cups water

sea salt

about 12 ice cubes, to serve

Above: A forest of Lebanese cedar trees, with Mount Hermon in the distance.

Serves 6–8

7g/¹/₄oz/2¹/₄ tsp dried yeast

2.5ml/¹/₂ tsp sugar

300ml/¹/₂ pint/1¹/₄ cups lukewarm water

450g/1lb/4 cups strong white bread flour, or a mixture of white and wholewheat flours

2.5ml/¹/₂ tsp salt

a little sunflower oil

Pitta bread
Khubz

Plain flat breads come in various guises throughout the Middle East, some with hollow pockets and some without. They are delicious when freshly baked or griddled and drizzled in butter or honey, and ideal, toasted, for dipping or as the base for grilled meat dishes. This is the standard bread dough in Lebanon, which is shaped to make different types of loaves.

1 In a small bowl, dissolve the yeast with the sugar in a little of the water and leave to cream for about 15 minutes, until frothy.

2 Sift the flour and salt into a bowl. Make a well in the centre and pour in the yeast mixture and the rest of the water. Draw the flour in and knead into a pliable dough.

3 Turn the dough on to a lightly floured surface and knead until it is smooth and elastic. Pour a drop of oil into the bowl and roll the dough in it to coat the surface. Cover the bowl with a damp cloth and leave to rise in a warm place for at least 2 hours, or overnight, until it has doubled in size.

4 Knock back (punch down) the dough and knead lightly. Divide into tangerine-sized balls and flatten with the palm of your hand. Dust a clean cloth with flour and place the flattened rounds of dough on it, leaving room to expand between them. Sprinkle with flour and lay another cloth on top. Leave to prove for 1–2 hours.

5 Preheat the oven to 230°C/450°F/Gas 8. Place several baking sheets in the oven to heat, then lightly oil them and place the bread rounds on them. Sprinkle with a little water and bake for 6–8 minutes – they should be lightly browned but not too firm, and slightly hollow inside.

6 Place the flat breads on a wire rack to cool a little before eating, or wrap them in a clean, dry cloth to keep them soft for eating later.

Energy 207kcal/877kJ; Protein 5.4g; Carbohydrate 44.5g, of which sugars 0.9g; Fat 2g, of which saturates 0.3g; Cholesterol 0mg; Calcium 80mg; Fibre 1.8g; Sodium 677mg

Little flat breads with thyme and sumac
Manakakeish bil zahtar

These spicy little breads are very popular to eat as a snack in the streets of Beirut and at neighbourhood bakeries, where they are often chosen for breakfast. They are great to serve freshly baked, either as a snack or as an accompaniment to a mezze spread.

1 In a small bowl, dissolve the yeast with the sugar in a little of the water and leave to cream for about 10 minutes until it begins to froth.

2 Sift the flour with the salt into a bowl and make a well in the centre. Pour the creamed yeast into the well with the rest of the water and draw the flour in from the sides to form a dough.

3 Turn the dough on to a floured surface and knead well for about 10 minutes, until it is smooth and elastic. Pour a drop of oil into the base of the bowl, roll the dough in it and cover with a damp cloth. Leave the dough to prove for about 2 hours, until it has doubled in size. Preheat the oven to 200°C/400°F/Gas 6.

4 In a small bowl, mix together the olive oil and the zahtar to make a paste.

5 Knock back (punch down) the dough, knead it lightly, then divide it into about 20 pieces. Knead each piece into a ball, flatten and stretch it, and smear it with some of the paste. Place the breads on lightly greased baking trays and bake them in the oven for about 10 minutes, until golden brown.

6 Sprinkle a little sea salt over the flat breads and serve them warm on their own, or to accompany other dishes.

Serves 4–6

7g/¹/₄oz/2¹/₄ tsp dried yeast

2.5ml/¹/₂ tsp sugar

300ml/¹/₂ pint/1¹/₄ cups lukewarm water

450g/1lb/4 cups strong white (bread) flour, or a mixture of white and wholewheat flours

2.5ml/¹/₂ tsp salt

30–45ml/2–3 tbsp olive oil, plus extra for oiling

45–60ml/3–4 tbsp zahtar

sea salt, for sprinkling

Cook's tip You can use the ready-prepared spice mix, zahtar, which is available in Middle Eastern stores, or make your own mix by combining 45ml/3 tbsp dried thyme with 15ml/1 tbsp sumac and 15ml/1 tbsp toasted sesame seeds.

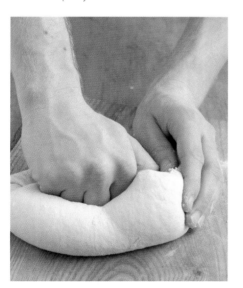  

Energy 310kcal/1314kJ; Protein 8.2g; Carbohydrate 60.9g, of which sugars 1.1g; Fat 5.6g, of which saturates 0.8g; Cholesterol 0mg; Calcium 119mg; Fibre 2.3g; Sodium 169mg

Bulgur and lamb patties
Kibbeh

Both the Lebanese and the Syrians claim kibbeh as their own. There are numerous variations – this one uses fragrant lamb and bulgur wheat.

1 Tip the bulgur into a bowl and pour in just enough boiling water to cover it. Cover the bowl with a clean dish towel and leave the bulgur for 20 minutes to swell.

2 Put the lamb into a food processor and grind to a paste. Turn it into a bowl and add the onion, spices and parsley, with salt and a generous amount of pepper.

3 Squeeze any excess water from the bulgur and grind it to a paste in the food processor. Add it to the bowl and use your hands to mix everything together and knead well. Process the mixture again and return it to the bowl for further kneading.

4 With wet hands, divide the mixture into small balls and flatten each one in the palm of your hand. Heat enough oil for frying in a shallow pan and cook the patties in batches, about 3 minutes on each side, until nicely browned. Drain on kitchen paper and serve hot with lemon wedges to squeeze over them.

Energy 407kcal/1694kJ; Protein 20.1g; Carbohydrate 35.9g, of which sugars 3.9g; Fat 20.9g, of which saturates 5.3g; Cholesterol 57mg; Calcium 65mg; Fibre 1.4g; Sodium 400mg

Serves 6

225g/8oz/1¼ cups bulgur, rinsed and drained

450g/1lb lean lamb, cut into small chunks

2 onions, grated

5–10ml/1–2 tsp ground allspice

5–10ml/1–2 tsp paprika

10ml/2 tsp ground cumin

5–10ml/1–2 tsp salt

small bunch of parsley, finely chopped

sunflower oil, for frying

ground black pepper

1–2 lemons, cut into wedges, to serve

Cook's tip Using wet hands to form the balls helps to prevent the mixture from sticking to them.

Serves 4–6

250g/9oz/1 cup dried broad (fava) beans, soaked overnight

115g/4oz/$\frac{1}{2}$ cup chickpeas, soaked overnight

10–15ml/2–3 tsp ground cumin

10ml/2 tsp ground coriander

1 red chilli, seeded and chopped

$\frac{1}{2}$ onion, chopped

1 red or green (bell) pepper, chopped

4 cloves garlic, crushed

small bunch of fresh coriander (cilantro), chopped

small bunch of flat leaf parsley, chopped

5ml/1 tsp bicarbonate of soda (baking soda)

sunflower oil for deep-frying

sea salt and ground black pepper

lemon wedges, to serve

Spicy bean balls
Felafel

Ideal street food, felafel are one of the most popular snacks in Lebanon and Egypt, eaten plain with pickles, or tucked into pitta bread with onions and yogurt. They can be served as a mezze dish with a tahini sauce, or with garlic-flavoured yogurt and lots of parsley, or with a salad.

1 Drain the beans and chickpeas and place in a blender with the dried spices. Blend to a thick purée, then add the chilli, onion, pepper, garlic and herbs. Whizz until smooth – add a little water if necessary – and season with salt and pepper.

2 Transfer the paste to a bowl, add the bicarbonate of soda and beat well to combine. Cover the bowl with a cloth and leave for 15 minutes.

3 With wet hands, mould the mixture into small, tight balls. Heat enough oil for deep-frying in a pan and fry the balls in batches until golden brown. Drain the felafel on kitchen paper and serve warm, with lemon wedges to squeeze over them.

Energy 303kcal/1282kJ; Protein 18.5g; Carbohydrate 44.7g, of which sugars 5.2g; Fat 6.9g, of which saturates 1.2g; Cholesterol 0mg; Calcium 88mg; Fibre 7.2g; Sodium 16mg

Above: A church on the snow-covered hills of Qadish Valley, Bakaa.

Serves 6

30ml/2 tbsp olive oil

1 onion, finely chopped

30ml/2 tbsp pine nuts

250g/9oz lean lamb, finely minced (ground)

10ml/2 tsp ground cinnamon

30ml/2 tbsp thick, strained yogurt

small bunch of flat leaf parsley, finely chopped

plain (all-purpose) flour, for dusting

450g/1lb ready-prepared puff pastry

sunflower oil, for frying

sea salt and ground black pepper

Cook's tip Instead of deep-frying, the pies can be baked in a preheated oven at 200°C/400°F/Gas 6. Arrange them on several baking trays lined with baking parchment and brush the tops with egg yolk beaten with a little water. You can also sprinkle them with sesame seeds, if you wish. Bake for 15–20 minutes, until puffed up and golden brown.

Lebanese meat pastries
Sambousak bi lahma

Little meat pastries are popular throughout the eastern Mediterranean region, varying only in the spices and herbs employed or in the shape of the pastry – which may be half-moon shaped, triangular or cigar-shaped. Perhaps the most popular of all the pastries, these meat-filled ones grace many mezze tables in Lebanon and are prepared for celebratory feasts.

1 Heat the olive oil in a heavy pan, stir in the chopped onion and cook until transparent but not browned. Add the pine nuts to the onions and just as they begin to colour, stir in the minced lamb.

2 Cook the lamb mixture for 4–5 minutes until all the meat is browned, stirring constantly. Stir in the cinnamon and season well with salt and pepper. Transfer the mixture to a large bowl, and leave to cool, then beat in the strained yogurt and chopped parsley.

3 Dust the work surface with a little flour and roll out the puff pastry thinly. Cut into 10cm/4in rounds or squares, depending on whether you want to create half-moon shapes or triangles. Place 10ml/2 tsp of the meat mixture just off centre, then pull the other side of the pastry over the filling so that the edges touch.

4 Using your finger, dampen the edges with water and pinch together to seal. You can create a pattern along the edge with a fork, if you like.

5 Heat enough oil in a pan for deep-frying and fry the pastries in batches for 5–6 minutes, until they are golden brown. Drain on kitchen paper and serve warm or at room temperature.

Energy 555kcal/2308kJ; Protein 14.5g; Carbohydrate 34.8g, of which sugars 4.4g; Fat 41.5g, of which saturates 4.3g; Cholesterol 32mg; Calcium 76mg; Fibre 0.9g; Sodium 275mg

Cheese and dill pastries
Sambousak bi jibneh

These little cheese pastries are best served hot so that the cheese is still soft and light and the pastry melts in the mouth. Ideal for snacks, parties, or a mezze spread, they are really versatile, as you can add any combination of herbs, crushed olives or chilli paste. If you use ready-prepared puff pastry, they are extremely easy to make.

1 Preheat the oven to 200°C/400°F/Gas 6. In a bowl, mash the feta with a fork. Grate the mozzarella or halloumi, or whizz to a paste in a blender or food processor, and add it to the feta. Mix in the chopped dill and beaten eggs, season with salt and pepper and mix together. Set aside while you prepare the pastry.

2 Dust the work surface with flour and roll out the pastry thinly. Using a round pastry cutter, or the rim of a cup, cut out as many 10cm/4in rounds as you can, then gather up the trimmings, reroll and cut out further rounds. Dust the pastry circles lightly with flour before stacking them.

3 Place 10ml/2 tsp of the cheese mixture just off centre on each pastry round. Lift the other side and bring it up over the filling until the edges touch each other to make a half-moon shape. Use your finger to dampen the edges with a little water and pinch them together to seal. For a more decorative effect, you can press along the edges with the back of a fork to make a pattern.

4 Line several baking trays with baking parchment and arrange the pastries on them. Brush the top of each pastry with a little of the beaten egg yolk mixture and place the trays in the oven. Bake for about 20 minutes, until the pastries are puffed up and golden brown. Serve immediately, while the cheese filling is warm.

Energy 526kcal/2192kJ; Protein 20.6g; Carbohydrate 30.5g, of which sugars 1.8g; Fat 37.4g, of which saturates 11.3g; Cholesterol 179mg; Calcium 352mg; Fibre 0.5g; Sodium 950mg

Above: The town of Ash Shamal nestles in the mountains of Kadisha Valley.

Serves 4–6

225g/8oz feta cheese, rinsed and drained

225g/8oz mozzarella or halloumi cheese

small bunch of fresh dill, chopped

2 eggs, lightly beaten

flour, for dusting

450g/1lb ready-prepared puff pastry

2 egg yolks, mixed with a little oil or water, for brushing

sea salt and ground black pepper

Spinach pastries with pine nuts
Fatayer bil sabanikh

Variations of these pastries are found throughout the eastern Mediterranean; in Lebanon, they are often prepared by the Christian communities for Lent.

1 Steam the spinach until wilted, then drain, refresh under running cold water and squeeze out the excess liquid with your hands. Chop the spinach coarsely.

2 Heat the oil and butter in a heavy pan and stir in the onion to soften. Add the pine nuts and cook for 2–3 minutes until the onions and pine nuts begin to turn golden. Stir in the spinach, sumac or lemon juice, and allspice and season well. Remove from the heat. Preheat the oven to 180°C/350°F/Gas 4.

3 Roll out the pastry on a lightly floured surface and cut out as many 10cm/4in rounds as you can. Spoon a little spinach mixture in the middle of each round and pull up the sides to make a pyramid by pinching the edges with your fingertips.

4 Line several baking trays with baking parchment and place the pastries on them. Brush the tops with a little oil and bake the pastries for about 30 minutes, until golden brown.

Energy 441kcal/1834kJ; Protein 9g; Carbohydrate 36.8g, of which sugars 7.2g; Fat 30.4g, of which saturates 2.3g; Cholesterol 6mg; Calcium 212mg; Fibre 3.1g; Sodium 371mg

Serves 6

500g/1¼lb fresh spinach, trimmed, washed and drained

30ml/2 tbsp olive oil, plus extra for brushing

15ml/1 tbsp butter

2 onions, chopped

45ml/3 tbsp pine nuts

15ml/1 tbsp ground sumac, or the juice of 1 lemon

5ml/1 tsp ground allspice

450g/1lb ready-prepared puff pastry

sea salt and ground black pepper

Cheese omelette with peppers and olives
Ljjit al jibne

This kind of thick omelette is often served as a snack, or cut into small portions as a mezze dish. On street stalls, omelettes are often cooked in large, wide pans and divided up for customers. They may be spiked with chillies or cumin and some include local Lebanese sausages.

1 Heat the oil in a heavy non-stick pan and cook the onion, peppers and chilli until they begin to brown. Stir in the feta cheese, olives and herbs and quickly add in the beaten eggs. Season with pepper.

2 Pull the egg mixture into the middle of the pan to help it spread and cook evenly. Reduce the heat, cover the pan with a lid, or a piece of foil, and let the omelette cook gently for 5–10 minutes until thick and solid.

3 At a street stall, the omelette would be served directly from the pan at this stage but, at home, you can drizzle a little extra oil over the top and brown it under a preheated grill (broiler), or in a hot oven, if you like. Cut the omelette into portions and serve hot or at room temperature.

Energy 303kcal/1252kJ; Protein 13.8g; Carbohydrate 5.5g, of which sugars 4.6g; Fat 25.4g, of which saturates 8.6g; Cholesterol 217mg; Calcium 230mg; Fibre 3.1g; Sodium 2304mg

Serves 4–6

30ml/2 tbsp olive oil

1 red onion, chopped

1 green or red (bell) pepper, chopped

1 red chilli, seeded and chopped

225g/8oz feta cheese, crumbled

12 black olives, pitted and halved

small bunch of flatleaf parsley, chopped

small bunch of mint leaves, chopped

6 eggs, lightly beaten with about 50ml/2fl oz/¼ cup milk

ground black pepper

GRAINS, BEANS & LENTILS

Roasted green wheat with chillies and pistachios

Bulgur with lamb and chickpeas

Brown lentils and rice with crispy onions

Green lentils with bulgur

Lebanese couscous

Saffron rice with pine nuts

Brown beans with onions, feta and parsley

Butter bean stew

Chickpeas with toasted bread and yogurt

Sustaining staples of the Lebanese table

No eastern Mediterranean household is complete without a little grain in the kitchen, enough to grind for bread and to prepare the much-loved kibbeh. Wheat has been the principal crop since ancient times and is at the root of many classic dishes. Rice is a more recent introduction: although there are records of it being used in some medieval culinary manuals, it was not until the Ottomans demanded rice from India and Egypt that it became widespread. For most Lebanese it is essential to produce rice, or some other grain, at every meal; if there is no grain, there must be sufficient bread.

Bulgur is a staple food of many peasant communities. Traditionally, it was prepared by boiling whole grains of wheat then spreading them on trays on the flat roofs to dry in the sun, before they were crushed into coarse, medium or fine grains. Another type of wheat, frikkeh, is harvested while still green and roasted to give it a unique nutty flavour; it is eaten with roasted meats and poultry. Couscous, which is more associated with North Africa, is found in some pockets of the eastern Mediterranean but is not very common. Pasta also appears in various guises in the region.

Lentils, beans and chickpeas have long been associated with the diet of the poor, but they are greatly enjoyed by everyone. Two of the best known Lebanese lentil dishes are mdardara, a rice pilaff with brown lentils and crispy onions, and imjadra, a spicy bulgur pilaff combined with red or green lentils. Beans, both fresh and dried, are perhaps even more popular than lentils. They have been a staple food since antiquity, and are still appreciated for their nutritional value, a fact summed up in the Arab saying, 'Beans have even satisfied the pharoahs.'

Roasted green wheat with chillies and pistachios
Frikkeh

Also known as freek, frikkeh is immature wheat that has been roasted in the husk to produce grain with a nutty texture and a mild smoky flavour. The green grains are cooked like ordinary wheat grains and served on their own or as an accompaniment to a main dish. In Lebanon, a popular method of preparing frikkeh is to simmer a whole chicken or shoulder of lamb in water to produce a stock, which is then used for cooking the frikkeh. The grains and the poached meat are served together.

Serves 4–6

30ml/2 tbsp ghee or 30ml/2 tbsp olive oil with a knob of butter

1 onion, finely sliced

2 cloves garlic, finely chopped

1–2 green chillies, seeded and finely sliced

115g/4oz/1 cup unsalted pistachios, halved

250g/9oz frikkeh, rinsed

900ml/1½ pints/3¾ cups well-flavoured chicken stock

30ml/2 tbsp pine nuts

sea salt and ground black pepper

creamy yogurt, to serve

Cook's tip An ancient food in Arab cuisine, frikkeh is highly nutritious, very high in fibre and with a low GI rating. It is now being produced commercially in other parts of the world as coarse grains as well as flakes, for use as a breakfast cereal, and milled into flour. Look for frikkeh in Middle Eastern and health food stores.

1 Heat the ghee, or olive oil and butter mixture, in a heavy pan and stir in the sliced onion, garlic and chillies. Cook until they begin to colour. Add the halved pistachios to the pan and fry for 1 minute, then stir in the frikkeh, coating it in the butter.

2 Pour in enough stock to just cover the mixture and bring it to the boil. Add salt and pepper to taste, reduce the heat and simmer for 15–20 minutes, until all the stock has been absorbed. Turn off the heat, cover the pan with a clean dish towel, followed by the lid, and leave the grains to steam for a further 10 minutes.

3 Meanwhile, put the pine nuts in a frying pan and dry-roast them over a medium heat, until golden brown. Remove from the heat and turn out on to a plate.

4 Turn the frikkeh into a warmed serving dish and sprinkle the pine nuts over the top. Serve immediately, with a dollop of creamy yogurt, as an accompaniment to any roasted or barbecued meat or poultry dish.

Energy 342kcal/1420kJ; Protein 8.7g; Carbohydrate 36.2g, of which sugars 3.2g; Fat 18.6g, of which saturates 2.2g; Cholesterol 0mg; Calcium 49mg; Fibre 1.7g; Sodium 226mg

Bulgur with lamb and chickpeas
Burghul bil lahma

Throughout the Lebanon, Syria, Jordan and Turkey, bulgur or cracked wheat is a staple ingredient. It is whole wheat, boiled until the grain is tender and the husk cracks open, then dried and ground, either coarsely or finely. There are many peasant dishes combining this much-loved grain with meat or chicken. Some recipes require the two ingredients to be cooked separately and then combined in a wide pan at the end; others call for both to be cooked together in the method of a pilaff. The Lebanese opt for the latter to produce this simple, hearty dish.

1 Rinse and drain the bulgur. Heat the ghee, or olive oil and butter mixture, in a heavy pan and add the chopped onion. Cook, stirring, until the onion softens and begins to turn a golden brown colour.

2 Stir the spices into the onions, and then toss in the chunks of lamb and stir to coat the meat in the butter and spices. Add the chickpeas and cook for 1 minute, then add the bulgur.

3 Pour in about 900ml/1½ pints/3¾ cups water and bring it to the boil. Season with salt and pepper and stir once.

4 Reduce the heat and simmer for 20 minutes, until all the water has been absorbed. Turn off the heat, cover the pan with a clean dish towel, followed by the lid, and leave the bulgur to steam for a further 10 minutes.

5 Turn the bulgur and lamb mixture into a serving dish and garnish with the chopped coriander. Serve immediately.

Energy 366kcal/1533kJ; Protein 18.5g; Carbohydrate 51.8g, of which sugars 2.7g; Fat 10.3g, of which saturates 2.5g; Cholesterol 25mg; Calcium 87mg; Fibre 4g; Sodium 46mg

Above: The distinctive rock formation known as Pigeon Rocks near Beirut.

Serves 4–6

30ml/2 tbsp ghee or 30ml/2 tbsp olive oil with a knob of butter

1 onion, finely chopped

5ml/1 tsp ground cumin

5ml/1 tsp ground fenugreek

200g/7oz lean lamb, cut into chunks

200g/7oz/1⅓ cups cooked chickpeas

250g/9oz/1½ cups coarse bulgur

sea salt and ground black pepper

small bunch of fresh coriander (cilantro), finely chopped, to garnish

Brown lentils and rice with crispy onions
Mdardara

This is an ancient classic and a great favourite in Lebanon. It is often served during Lent among the Christian communities, whereas for Muslims it is an essential part of the main meal served to break the fast during Ramadan.

1 Bring a pan of water to the boil and toss in the lentils. Boil rapidly for 10–15 minutes, until the lentils are tender but still firm. Drain and refresh under cold water.

2 Heat the oil or ghee in a heavy pan and cook the onions with the sugar for 3–4 minutes, until they begin to turn golden. Add the spices and cook for 1–2 minutes, then add the lentils and rice, tossing to coat the grains in the spicy onion mixture.

3 Add water to just cover the lentils and rice, and bring to the boil. Reduce the heat and simmer gently for about 15 minutes, until the water has been absorbed. Turn off the heat, cover the pan with a clean dish towel, followed by the lid, and leave the rice and lentils to steam for a further 10 minutes.

4 Meanwhile, prepare the crispy onions. Heat the oil in a deep frying pan and fry the onions until brown and crisp, then drain on kitchen paper. Turn the rice into a serving dish, season and fluff up with a fork. Sprinkle with cinnamon and spoon the onions on top. Serve immediately with yogurt, or with any meat, poultry or fish dish.

Energy 411kcal/1717kJ; Protein 13.7g; Carbohydrate 58.3g, of which sugars 7g; Fat 14.3g, of which saturates 1.8g; Cholesterol 0mg; Calcium 68mg; Fibre 5g; Sodium 9mg

Serves 4–6

225g/8oz/1 cup brown lentils, rinsed

45–60ml/3–4 tbsp olive oil or ghee

2 onions, finely chopped

5ml/1 tsp sugar

5ml/1 tsp ground coriander

5ml/1 tsp ground cumin

225g/8oz/generous 1 cup long grain rice, well rinsed

sea salt and ground black pepper

5ml/1 tsp ground cinnamon, to garnish

For the crispy onions

sunflower oil for deep-frying

2 onions, halved lengthways and sliced with the grain

Green lentils with bulgur
Imjadra

Similar to mdardara, this is one of Lebanon's lesser known countryside specialities. It combines lentils with a grain to produce a wholesome dish that can be served on its own, or with any meat, poultry or fish dish.

1 Bring a pan of water to the boil, add the lentils and cook for about 15 minutes, until they are tender but not soft or mushy. Drain and refresh under cold water.

2 Heat the ghee in a heavy pan, stir in the onion and cook until it begins to colour. Add the cumin seeds and stir in the bulgur, coating it in the ghee. Stir in the lentils and pour in the stock.

3 Season with salt and pepper and bring to the boil. Reduce the heat and simmer for 15 minutes. Turn off the heat and place a clean dish towel over the pan, followed by the lid. Leave the bulgur and lentils to steam for 10 minutes.

4 Meanwhile, melt the butter in a small pan. Turn the rice and lentils into a serving dish, pour the melted butter over the top and garnish with the coriander and mint.

Energy 306kcal/1284kJ; Protein 13.8g; Carbohydrate 52.8g, of which sugars 4.2g; Fat 5.4g, of which saturates 0.6g; Cholesterol 0mg; Calcium 63mg; Fibre 4.3g; Sodium 9mg

Serves 4–6

225g/8oz/1 cup green lentils, rinsed

30ml/2 tbsp ghee, or olive oil with a knob of butter

2 onions, finely chopped

5–10ml/1–2 tsp cumin seeds

225g/8oz/1¼ cups coarse bulgur, rinsed

900ml/1½ pints/3¾ cups stock or water

sea salt and ground black pepper

To serve

15ml/1 tbsp ghee or butter

small bunch of fresh coriander (cilantro), coarsely chopped

small bunch of mint, coarsely chopped

Above: A traditional-style four-storey building in the heart of Beirut.

Serves 6

450g/1lb/2½ cups couscous, rinsed and drained

30ml/2 tbsp ghee, or 30ml/2 tbsp olive oil with a knob of butter

1 onion, finely chopped

2–3 cloves garlic, finely chopped

1 red or green chilli, seeded and very finely chopped

1 medium carrot, finely diced

5–10ml/1–2 tsp ground cinnamon

small bunch of fresh coriander (cilantro), finely chopped

sea salt and ground black pepper

For the stock

1 small organic chicken

2 onions, quartered

2 cinnamon sticks

4 cardamom pods

4 cloves

2 bay leaves

Lebanese couscous
Moghrabiyeh

Although couscous is most closely associated with the culinary cultures of North Africa, it is also enjoyed in Lebanon, Syria and Jordan, where it is called mograbiyeh, meaning 'from the Maghreb'.

1 Place the chicken in a deep pan with the other stock ingredients and cover with water. Bring the water to the boil, reduce the heat and simmer for 1 hour, or until the chicken is tender. Transfer the chicken to a plate. Strain the stock, return it to the pan and boil it over a high heat for about 30 minutes, to reduce.

2 Remove and discard the skin from the chicken and tear the flesh into thin strips, or cut it into bitesize chunks. Cover the chicken and keep warm.

3 Tip the couscous into a bowl and pour in about 500ml/17fl oz/2 cups warm water. Add 5ml/1 tsp salt, stir the couscous once, then place a clean dish towel over the bowl and leave for 10 minutes for the couscous to swell.

4 Meanwhile, heat the ghee or olive oil and butter in a heavy, shallow pan and stir in the onions and garlic. Cook for a minute to soften, then add the chilli and carrot and sauté for 2–3 minutes, until they begin to colour.

5 Stir the cinnamon and half the coriander into the onion mixture, then add the couscous, forking through it constantly to mix well and make sure the grains don't clump together, until it is heated through.

6 Turn the couscous into a warmed serving dish and arrange the shredded chicken on top. Season the reduced stock with salt and pepper and spoon some of it over the chicken to moisten. Garnish with the remaining coriander and pour the rest of the stock into a bowl for spooning over individual portions.

Energy 376kcal/1574kJ; Protein 31.9g; Carbohydrate 44.6g, of which sugars 4g; Fat 8.8g, of which saturates 3.5g; Cholesterol 70mg; Calcium 49mg; Fibre 1.1g; Sodium 128mg

Serves 4

45ml/3 tbsp butter or ghee

225g/8oz/generous 1 cup long grain rice

good pinch of saffron fronds

600ml/1 pint/2¹⁄₂ cups chicken stock
or water

30ml/2 tbsp pine nuts

sea salt and ground black pepper

Cook's tip Saffron may be expensive,
but it is worth it. The colour and gentle
aroma it imparts is unique, and is ideal
for a mildly-flavoured dish such as this.

Saffron rice with pine nuts
Ruz bi za'faran

Although rice is relatively new to Lebanon it plays a huge role in the diet, and
a dish of rice will appear at almost every meal. This dish, tinted gold with
saffron, is ideal for serving with grilled fish or roasted meat or poultry.

1 Melt 30ml/2 tbsp of the butter or ghee in a heavy pan. Stir in the rice and saffron,
making sure the grains are coated in butter. Pour in the stock, season with salt and
pepper, and bring to the boil. Reduce the heat and simmer for 15 minutes, until all
the water has been absorbed, then turn off the heat and cover the pan with a clean
dish towel, followed by the lid. Leave to steam for a further 10 minutes.

2 Meanwhile, melt the remaining butter in a frying pan. Stir in the pine nuts and
cook until they turn golden. Drain them on kitchen paper.

3 Fluff up the rice with a fork and turn it on to a serving dish. Sprinkle the pine nuts
over the top and serve immediately.

Energy 316kcal/1316kJ; Protein 5.5g; Carbohydrate 45.2g, of which sugars 0.3g; Fat 12.5g, of which
saturates 5g; Cholesterol 20mg; Calcium 13mg; Fibre 0.2g; Sodium 246mg

Brown beans with onions, feta and parsley
Foul medames

Traditionally a peasant dish with its origins in ancient Egypt, foul medames is a popular staple dish in Lebanon, Syria and Jordan. It is generally served for breakfast or as part of a mezze spread.

1 Drain the beans and place them in a deep pot filled with water. Bring the water to the boil, reduce the heat and simmer the beans for about 1 hour, until they are tender but not soft or mushy.

2 When the beans are almost cooked, prepare the accompaniments and pile each one into a small bowl. Drain the beans and, while they are still warm, transfer them into a large serving bowl and add the olive oil, garlic and cumin. Squeeze in the lemon juice, season with salt and pepper and mix well.

3 Serve the warm beans immediately, accompanied by the bowls of red onions, feta and parsley, to which everyone helps themselves.

Energy 200kcal/846kJ; Protein 13.6g; Carbohydrate 27.3g, of which sugars 1.5g; Fat 4.8g, of which saturates 0.7g; Cholesterol 0mg; Calcium 65mg; Fibre 9.4g; Sodium 12mg

Serves 4–6

250g/9oz/1¼ cups dried broad (fava) beans, soaked overnight

30–45ml/2–3 tbsp olive oil

2 cloves garlic, crushed

5–10ml/1–2 tsp cumin seeds, dry roasted and crushed

juice of 1 lemon

sea salt and ground black pepper

To serve

1–2 red onions, halved lengthways, halved again crossways, and finely sliced with the grain

225/8oz feta cheese, diced or crumbled

bunch of flat leaf parsley, roughly chopped

Butter bean stew
Fassoulia baida

As beans are cheap, nourishing and readily available, there are times when a stew like this may constitute the main meal of the day. Some include meat or root vegetables, but this version simply contains beans and is best served with a dollop of yogurt and bread to mop up the sauce.

1 Drain the beans and transfer them into a pan filled with water. Bring to the boil, reduce the heat and simmer the beans for about 45 minutes, until tender but retaining a bite. Drain, refresh in cold water, and remove any loose skins.

2 Heat the oil and butter in a heavy pan and cook the onions, garlic and sugar for 2–3 minutes, until they begin to colour. Add the spices and toss in the beans. Add the tomatoes and cook over a medium heat for about 20 minutes.

3 Season the stew with salt and pepper and stir in half the coriander. Remove the cinnamon and transfer the beans into a serving bowl. Garnish with the remaining coriander and serve with bread, or as an accompaniment to a meat or grain dish.

Energy 295kcal/1251kJ; Protein 18.8g; Carbohydrate 45.4g, of which sugars 11.5g; Fat 5.7g, of which saturates 0.9g; Cholesterol 0mg; Calcium 108mg; Fibre 14.1g; Sodium 29mg

Serves 4–6

450/1lb/2½ cups dried butter (lima) beans, soaked overnight

30ml/2 tbsp olive oil with a knob of butter, or 30ml/2 tbsp ghee

2 onions, finely chopped

4–6 cloves garlic, crushed

10ml/2 tsp sugar

10ml/2 tsp cumin seeds

10ml/2 tsp coriander seeds

1 large cinnamon stick

2 x 400g/14oz cans chopped tomatoes

small bunch of fresh coriander (cilantro), coarsely chopped

sea salt and ground black pepper

Serves 4

225g/8oz/1¼ cups chickpeas, soaked overnight

600ml/1 pint/2½ cups creamy, strained yogurt

2–3 cloves garlic, crushed

4 pitta breads, toasted

5–10ml/1–2 tsp dried mint

5ml/1 tsp paprika

15ml/1 tbsp butter

30ml/2 tbsp pine nuts

sea salt and ground black pepper

Chickpeas with toasted bread and yogurt
Fattet hummus

A number of popular dishes fall into the fatta category, an Arabic term denoting the breaking of toasted flat bread into pieces to provide a bed for the other ingredients. This simple dish of chickpeas is a street favourite.

1 Drain the chickpeas and transfer them into a pot. Cover with plenty of water and bring it to the boil. Reduce the heat and simmer for 1 hour, until tender. Drain, reserving several spoonfuls of the cooking liquid.

2 Beat the yogurt with the garlic and season with salt and pepper. Break up the toasted bread into bitesize pieces and arrange them on a serving dish. Spread the chickpeas over the bread and moisten with the cooking liquid. Spoon the yogurt generously on to the top and sprinkle with the dried mint and paprika.

3 Quickly melt the butter in a frying pan and fry the pine nuts until they turn golden. Sprinkle them over the top of the yogurt and serve immediately.

Energy 354kcal/1489kJ; Protein 21.5g; Carbohydrate 41.1g, of which sugars 13.1g; Fat 13g, of which saturates 3.4g; Cholesterol 11mg; Calcium 380mg; Fibre 6.5g; Sodium 175mg

FISH & SHELLFISH

Fried red mullet with pitta bread

Poached fish with rice and pine nuts

Charcoal-grilled trout with garlic, lemon and zahtar

Baked fish with bay leaves, oranges and limes

Roasted fish with chillies and walnuts

Fried sardines with lemon

Fish with tomato and pomegranate sauce

Fish kibbeh with an onion filling

Tangy prawn and pepper kebabs

Sautéed prawns with coriander and lime

Highly prized harvest of the seas

In the early cooking manuals of the eastern Mediterranean, recipes rarely specified a type of fish to be used because people would use whatever fish was available. Inland, that was more likely to be of the freshwater variety, but Lebanon has a fairly extensive coastline that yields a varied catch. The most popular fish include sea bass, red snapper, garfish, hake, grouper, sardine, swordfish, tuna, grey and red mullet (the latter being a species favoured by the Romans), and sole. Freshwater fish, such as trout, eel, carp and barbel, end up in the rural markets. Most firm-fleshed fish are interchangeable in soups, kibbeh and stews, and are ideal for barbecuing and baking. The most common way of cooking fish is to grill it over charcoal or bake it in the oven and serve it with a tahini sauce, lemon wedges or herbs. Fish is rarely cooked with milk or served with yogurt, as there is a widespread belief that such a combination could render it harmful.

The roe of grey mullet was once so highly prized in the eastern Mediterranean that it was almost as valuable as caviar from the Caspian Sea. The Arabs enjoyed a delicacy called batarekh, which involved salting, pressing and drying the roe, then encasing it in beeswax. The Lebanese still preserve the roe in this manner and serve it cut into very thin slices, drizzled with a little olive oil and a splash of lemon juice. Preserving fish is an ancient tradition and a very practical one. Whole fish or boned fillets are hung up on makeshift lines to dry, then rubbed in salt. The Orontes River in Lebanon made a name for itself during the Ottoman period as a locale for salt-cured fish. Nowadays, salted fish are considered a delicacy rather than a necessity, and are often eaten with bread as cheese or pâté might be eaten elsewhere.

Serves 4

4 red mullet, about 250g/9oz each, gutted, scaled and cleaned

15–30ml/1–2 tbsp plain (all-purpose) flour

2 pitta breads

olive, sunflower, or groundnut (peanut) oil for frying

sea salt and ground black pepper

small bunch of flat leaf parsley, coarsely chopped, to garnish

1 lemon, cut into quarters, to serve

For the tahini sauce

1–2 cloves garlic

150ml/$\frac{1}{4}$ pint/$\frac{2}{3}$ cup smooth tahini

juice of 1 lemon

juice of 1 small orange

sea salt and ground black pepper

Variation If red mullet is not available, you can also use red snapper or sea bass for this recipe.

Fried red mullet with pitta bread
Sultan Ibrahim mikli

Red mullet is regarded as a fish of distinction in Lebanon. Splendidly pink and succulent, the fresh fish are caught daily and invariably grilled or fried. In this classic dish the fried fish is covered with crisp, golden strips of pitta bread and served with a tahini sauce.

1 First prepare the tahini sauce. Pound the garlic cloves in a mortar and pestle with a little salt, until you have a smooth paste.

2 Beat the tahini paste in a bowl with the lemon and orange juices, until the mixture is thick and smooth with the consistency of pouring cream. Beat in the garlic paste, and season to taste with salt and pepper. Set aside.

3 Rinse the mullet under cold running water and pat dry inside and out with kitchen paper. Using a sharp knife, slash each fish with three diagonal cuts on each side. Sprinkle with salt and pepper and toss them in flour so that they are lightly coated. Cut the pitta bread into strips.

4 Heat enough oil for frying in a heavy pan and cook the fish, two at a time, for about 3 minutes on each side, until they are crisp and golden. Drain on kitchen paper and keep warm.

5 Toss the strips of pitta bread in the same oil, until they too are crisp and golden, and drain them on kitchen paper.

6 Arrange the fish on a serving dish, drizzle a little tahini sauce over them, garnish with the parsley, and sprinkle the pitta strips over the top. Serve immediately with lemon wedges to squeeze over them and the rest of the tahini sauce.

Energy 556kcal/2318kJ; Protein 35.1g; Carbohydrate 23.9g, of which sugars 1.2g; Fat 36.2g, of which saturates 4.4g; Cholesterol 0mg; Calcium 386mg; Fibre 4.2g; Sodium 329mg

Poached fish with rice and pine nuts
Sayadieh samak

Originally a simple dish prepared by fishermen, this recipe has become more sophisticated and now ranks with the Lebanese classics. In restaurants in coastal areas, it is often served as the plat du jour, whereas in homes it is prepared as a special dish to honour guests.

1 Heat the oil in a heavy pan and fry the onions for 5–10 minutes, until dark brown. Turn off the heat and set aside.

2 Rub the fish with salt inside and out. Place the parsley leaves in the base of a pan, lay the fish on top and add the bay leaves, cinnamon stick and peppercorns. Just cover with water and bring to the boil. Reduce the heat and simmer gently for about 5 minutes. Transfer the fish to a board and leave it to cool a little, remove the skin, take the flesh off the bone and break into bitesize pieces. Cover with foil.

3 Return the skin, head and bones to the cooking liquid and bring to the boil. Reduce the heat and bubble for 15–20 minutes, to reduce by half. Strain the stock, return it to the pan and bring it to the boil.

4 Add the browned onions to the stock, and simmer for a further 10–15 minutes. Using a slotted spoon, lift out the onions and press them through a sieve (strainer) back into the pot. Stir well and season. Return to the boil, add the rice, cumin and cinnamon and simmer for 10 minutes, until the rice has absorbed the stock. Turn off the heat, cover the pan with a clean dish towel, followed by the lid, and leave to steam for a further 10 minutes.

5 Turn the rice into a serving dish, stir a little of the fish into it and sprinkle the rest on top. Dry roast the pine nuts in a pan over a medium heat until golden and sprinkle them over the top. Dust with cinnamon and serve with lemon wedges.

Above: Fishing boats moored in the harbour of Tyre in Southern Lebanon.

Serves 4–6

30–45ml/2–3 tbsp olive oil

2 onions, finely sliced

1 firm-fleshed fish, such as sea bass or trout (about 900g/2lb), scaled, gutted and cleaned

bunch of flat leaf parsley

2–3 bay leaves

1 cinnamon stick

6 black peppercorns

250g/9oz/1¼ cups long grain rice, well rinsed and drained

5–10ml/1–2 tsp ground cumin

5–10ml/1–2 tsp ground cinnamon, plus extra for dusting

30ml/2 tbsp pine nuts

sea salt

1 lemon, cut into wedges, to serve

Cook's tip If you don't have a pan large enough to poach the fish whole, cut it into two or three pieces to fit. Or transfer the fish and stock to a roasting pan and bake in the oven.

Energy 385kcal/1611kJ; Protein 28.3g; Carbohydrate 40.6g, of which sugars 4.9g; Fat 12.2g, of which saturates 1.8g; Cholesterol 96mg; Calcium 68mg; Fibre 1.3g; Sodium 90mg

Serves 4

juice of 2 lemons

4 cloves garlic, crushed

4 small trout (about 300g/11oz each), gutted and cleaned

10ml/2 tsp zahtar

sea salt

ground pink peppercorns

1 lemon, cut into wedges, to serve

Variation Small whole sea bass can also be used instead of trout in this recipe.

Charcoal-grilled trout with garlic, lemon and zahtar
Samak meshwi

The traditional method of cooking fish in the eastern Mediterranean is over charcoal or wood embers. Whether it is sea or freshwater fish, the flesh is always tasty and juicy cooked this way.

1 Prepare the barbecue (or preheat a ridged griddle). In a bowl, mix together the lemon juice and crushed garlic.

2 Using a sharp knife, score the flesh of the fish diagonally three times on each side. Rub a little salt and pepper into the fish, inside and out.

3 Brush one side of the fish with the lemon juice and place it, lemon-juice side down, on an oiled rack set over the glowing coals. Brush the rest of the lemon juice on the other side and grill the fish for about 4 minutes on each side.

4 Transfer the fish to a serving dish. Sprinkle the zahtar over the top and serve immediately with lemon wedges to squeeze over them.

Energy 279kcal/1176kJ; Protein 47.3g; Carbohydrate 1.7g, of which sugars 0.1g; Fat 9.4g, of which saturates 2.2g; Cholesterol 192mg; Calcium 78mg; Fibre 0.2g; Sodium 175mg

Baked fish with bay leaves, oranges and limes
Tajin samak

Until recently many households in Lebanon lacked ovens. Instead, once a week or so a freshly caught fish might be taken along to the communal neighbourhood oven to be baked simply, as in this recipe. Serve the baked fish with a salad or a tahini sauce.

1 Whisk together all the ingredients for the marinade. Place the fish in a dish and pour the marinade over it. Cover and chill for 1–2 hours. Preheat the oven to 180°C/350°F/Gas 4.

2 Transfer the fish to an ovenproof dish and spoon the marinade over it. Tuck the bay leaves under it and arrange several slices of orange and lime alternately along the inside, and on top, of the fish.

3 Cover the dish with foil and bake for 15 minutes. Remove the foil, dot the fish with butter and bake uncovered for a further 10 minutes. Serve immediately.

Energy 257kcal/1078kJ; Protein 35g; Carbohydrate 1.1g, of which sugars 1.1g; Fat 12.6g, of which saturates 4g; Cholesterol 153mg; Calcium 56mg; Fibre 0g; Sodium 160mg

Serves 4

1 sea bass or grouper (weighing about 900g/2lb), gutted and cleaned

2–3 bay leaves

1 lime, finely sliced

1 small orange, finely sliced

15ml/1 tbsp butter

For the marinade

juice of 2 oranges

juice of 2 limes

30ml/2 tbsp olive oil

1 clove garlic, crushed

sea salt and ground black pepper

Roasted fish with chillies and walnuts
Samak harra

This simple dish is a favourite along the coast of Lebanon, particularly around Tripoli. Traditionally dogfish is used, but any firm-fleshed fish, such as trout, sea bass or snapper, is ideal. Topped with a spicy tahini sauce, this dish is spectacular when garnished with fresh pomegranate seeds.

1 Preheat the oven to 200°C/400°F/Gas 6. Using a sharp knife, make three or four diagonal slits on each side of the fish. Rub the cavity with salt and pepper, cover the fish and chill for 30 minutes.

2 Meanwhile, prepare the filling. Heat 30ml/2 tbsp olive oil in a heavy pan and fry the onions, pepper, and chillies until lightly browned. Stir in the walnuts and pomegranate molasses and add half the coriander and parsley. Season to taste and leave the filling to cool.

3 Fill the fish with the stuffing and secure the opening with a wooden skewer or cocktail sticks (toothpicks). Place the fish in an oiled baking dish and pour over the remaining oil. Bake in the preheated oven for about 30 minutes.

4 Meanwhile, to make the sauce, beat the tahini with the lemon and orange juice, adding a little water if necessary, until the mixture is smooth and creamy. Heat the olive oil in a small frying pan and stir in the garlic and chillies, until they begin to colour. Stir in the tahini mixture and heat it through. Season with salt and pepper and keep the sauce warm.

5 Transfer the cooked fish to a serving dish and drizzle some of the sauce over the top. Garnish with the pomegranate seeds and serve immediately with the rest of the sauce served separately.

Serves 4

2 x 900g/2lb firm-fleshed fish, gutted and cleaned

60ml/4 tbsp olive oil

2 onions, finely chopped

1 green (bell) pepper, finely chopped

1–2 red chillies, seeded and very finely chopped

115g/4oz walnuts, finely chopped

15–30ml/1–2 tbsp pomegranate molasses

small bunch of fresh coriander (cilantro), finely chopped

small bunch of flat leaf parsley, finely chopped

sea salt and ground black pepper

For the sauce

60ml/4 tbsp tahini

juice of 1 lemon

juice of 1 orange

15ml/1 tbsp olive oil

2 cloves garlic, finely chopped

1–2 red chillies, seeded and chopped

sea salt and ground black pepper

seeds of ½ pomegranate, with pith removed, to garnish

Energy 772kcal/3223kJ; Protein 78.8g; Carbohydrate 13.1g, of which sugars 10.3g; Fat 45.3g, of which saturates 6.5g; Cholesterol 288mg; Calcium 292mg; Fibre 4.9g; Sodium 276mg

Fried sardines with lemon
Sardin makli

This simple street dish is generally made with small sardines or sprats. Often the whole fish are dipped in flour and fried in pans beside the moored fishing boats and bustling fish markets. The locals enjoy them this way, popping them whole into their mouths. For a western palate, they are better gutted and are particularly delicious if steeped in lemon juice or beer before frying.

1 If you are marinating the fish, place them in a shallow dish and pour the beer over them. Cover and chill for 1–2 hours, then drain and pat dry.

2 Rub the fish with a little salt and pepper and dip them in the flour until lightly coated. Heat enough oil for deep-frying in a heavy pan.

3 Fry the fish in batches for 5–6 minutes, until crisp and golden. Drain them on kitchen paper and serve hot, with lemon halves to squeeze over them.

Energy 358kcal/1488kJ; Protein 18.7g; Carbohydrate 11.7g, of which sugars 0.2g; Fat 26.5g, of which saturates 4.4g; Cholesterol 0mg; Calcium 107mg; Fibre 0.5g; Sodium 96mg

Serves 4

450g/1lb fresh small sardines, gutted and cleaned

300ml/½ pint/1¼ cups beer (optional)

60–75ml/4–5 tbsp chickpea or plain (all-purpose) flour

olive or sunflower oil for deep frying

sea salt and ground black pepper

2 lemons, halved, to serve

Serves 4

900g/2lb firm-fleshed fish fillets

45–60ml/3–4 tbsp olive oil

juice of 1 lemon

2–3 cloves garlic, finely chopped

4 tomatoes, skinned, seeded, and chopped

15ml/1 tbsp pomegranate molasses

10ml/2 tsp sugar

sea salt and ground black pepper

small bunch of fresh parsley, finely chopped, to garnish

Cook's tip Pomegranate molasses, sometimes sold as pomegranate syrup, is available from Middle Eastern stores and some delicatessens and supermarkets.

Fish with tomato and pomegranate sauce
Tajin samak bi banadura

This is a tasty method of cooking any firm-fleshed fish, such as large sardines, sea bass, red snapper, grouper and trout. The pomegranate molasses adds a tangy, sour note to the sauce and enriches the colour.

1 Preheat the oven to 180°C/350°F/Gas 4. Arrange the fish in an ovenproof dish, rub with salt and pepper and pour over 30ml/2 tbsp olive oil and the lemon juice. Cover with foil and bake for about 25 minutes, until the fish is cooked.

2 Meanwhile, heat the rest of the oil in a heavy frying pan. Fry the garlic until it begins to colour, then add the tomatoes. Cook for 5 minutes, then stir in the pomegranate molasses with the sugar. Reduce the heat and cook gently until the sauce thickens. Season with salt and pepper. Keep warm until the fish is ready.

3 Arrange the fish on a serving dish, spoon the sauce over and around the fish and sprinkle with the parsley.

Energy 284kcal/1192kJ; Protein 41.7g; Carbohydrate 6.9g, of which sugars 6.9g; Fat 10.1g, of which saturates 1.5g; Cholesterol 104mg; Calcium 28mg; Fibre 0.8g; Sodium 149mg

Fish kibbeh with an onion filling
Kibbeh samak

This kibbeh is traditionally prepared in the coastal towns to mark special events. Among the Christian communities it is a dish that most families prepare for Lent. Any firm-fleshed fish, including haddock and cod, can be used for this recipe. The kibbeh can also be served as a mezze dish if you mould the mixture into tiny bitesize balls.

1 First prepare the filling. Heat the oil in a small frying pan, stir in the onions and cook until they soften and begin to colour. Add the cinnamon and orange rind, stir through to mix together and season with salt and pepper. Set aside.

2 Place the bulgur in a bowl and pour over enough boiling water to just cover. Place a clean dish towel over the bowl and leave the bulgur for about 10 minutes to absorb the water and expand.

3 Squeeze the bulgur to drain off any excess water and place it in a blender or food processor with the chopped onion, fish fillets, turmeric and coriander. Whizz the mixture to a paste and season with salt and pepper.

4 With wet hands, take a small portion of the kibbeh mixture and mould it into the shape of an egg. Hollow out the egg with a finger and fill the cavity with a little of the onion mixture. Pinch the edges of the kibbeh together to seal in the filling and form an egg shape once more. Repeat with the rest of the mixture.

5 Heat enough oil for shallow frying in a heavy pan. Roll the kibbeh lightly in flour and fry them in batches until golden brown. Drain them on kitchen paper and serve hot with wedges of lemon to squeeze over them.

Above: Roman remains at Fakra, with snow-topped mountains in the distance.

Serves 4

For the filling

15–30ml/1–2 tbsp olive oil

2 onions, finely chopped

5ml/1 tsp ground cinnamon

grated rind of 1/2 orange

sea salt and ground black pepper

For the kibbeh

175g/6oz/1 cup fine bulgur, well rinsed and drained

1 onion, finely chopped

450g/1lb boneless fish fillets

5–10ml/1–2 tsp ground turmeric

small bunch of fresh coriander (cilantro), finely chopped

flour for dusting

sunflower oil for frying

sea salt and ground black pepper

1 lemon, cut into wedges, to serve

Energy 453kcal/1884kJ; Protein 29.7g; Carbohydrate 22.8g, of which sugars 11.5g; Fat 27.7g, of which saturates 9.7g; Cholesterol 93mg; Calcium 231mg; Fibre 1.1g; Sodium 178mg

Serves 4

15ml/1 tbsp pomegranate molasses

15ml/1 tbsp olive oil

juice of 1 lemon

2 cloves garlic, crushed

10ml/2 tsp sugar

16 large raw prawns (jumbo shrimp), shelled and deveined

2 green (bell) peppers, cut into bitesize chunks

sea salt

Tangy prawn and pepper kebabs
Kreidess kebab

A popular shellfish dish prepared in the fishing villages, prawn kebabs are simple and satisfying, served with a rice dish and salad. Generally, they are prepared with green pepper in Lebanon, but variations are made with other shellfish, tomato, and onion throughout the eastern Mediterranean.

1 In a large bowl, mix together the pomegranate molasses, olive oil, lemon juice, garlic and sugar. Season the mixture with salt. Add the prawns to the mixture, and toss gently, making sure they are all well coated with the marinade. Cover the dish and chill for 1–2 hours.

2 Prepare the barbecue, if using, or preheat a griddle or grill (broiler). Thread the marinated prawns on to four skewers, alternately with the pepper pieces.

3 Grill the kebabs for 2–3 minutes on each side, basting with any leftover marinade. Serve immediately.

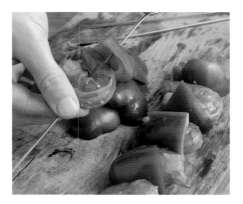

Energy 102kcal/427kJ; Protein 9.7g; Carbohydrate 8.6g, of which sugars 8.3g; Fat 3.4g, of which saturates 0.5g; Cholesterol 98mg; Calcium 48mg; Fibre 1.4g; Sodium 109mg

Sautéed prawns with coriander and lime
Kreidess mikli

Freshly caught large prawns cooked simply in this manner are delicious. There are many versions of this dish throughout the eastern Mediterranean, but this is served in the picturesque fishing villages up the coast from Beirut.

1 Heat the oil in a heavy pan, toss in the crushed garlic and cook, stirring constantly, until it begins to colour.

2 Add the lime rind, toss in the prawns, and stir-fry until they begin to turn pink. Add the lime juice and coriander and season with salt, and let the liquid sizzle before removing from the heat. Eat immediately with your fingers.

Energy 106kcal/442kJ; Protein 11.8g; Carbohydrate 1.2g, of which sugars 0.4g; Fat 6.1g, of which saturates 0.9g; Cholesterol 122mg; Calcium 75mg; Fibre 0.8g; Sodium 123mg

Serves 3–4

30–45ml/2–3 tbsp olive oil

2–3 cloves garlic, crushed

rind and juice of 1 lime

15–16 raw king prawns (jumbo shrimp), peeled to the tails and deveined

small bunch of fresh coriander (cilantro), roughly chopped

sea salt

MEAT & POULTRY

Baked kibbeh with onions and pine nuts

Baked lamb and potato pie

Spicy meat dumplings with yogurt

Pasha's meatballs in tomato sauce

Lamb stew with plums

Dervish's beads

Roasted leg of lamb with rice

Roasted onions stuffed with lamb

Stuffed artichoke bottoms

Lamb and vegetable stew

Aromatic chicken on toasted pitta bread

Roasted stuffed turkey with thyme

Sizzling, aromatic and bursting with flavour

Hunting once played an important role in the lives of both poor and rich in Lebanon, and animals such as rabbit, hare, gazelle, wild boar, porcupine, and a variety of game birds were hunted. Poultry was highly regarded in the medieval Arab kitchen, and numerous chicken recipes are recorded, some including rhubarb, mulberries, almonds, walnuts and pomegranates. The list of exotic and interesting recipes was extended during the Ottoman period and the Ottomans also introduced turkey from the New World. Muslims have to adhere to certain restrictions regarding meat. The Qur'an forbids any form of pork, or the consumption of an animal's blood, and slaughtering has to follow certain guidelines for it to be passed as permissable, or 'halal', meat.

Throughout the history of the eastern Mediterranean the preferred meat has traditionally been mutton or lamb. The most highly prized breed is the Awassi, as it produces excellent meat and the fat stored in its tail is much sought after as a pungent cooking fat, aliya, which lends its flavour to many dishes. The addition of beef and veal to the diet is relatively recent. Traditionally, cows and oxen were valued solely for their milk and labour in the fields but nowadays beef is often substituted for lamb in stews and meatballs.

Modern daily fare includes a variety of meat stews, and kibbeh are prepared daily. Street vendors serve shawarma, the Arab equivalent of Turkish döner, eaten in a pocket of pitta bread, smothered in tahini or yogurt, with onions, tomatoes, pickles and herbs. For special occasions a whole lamb roasted on a spit, quzi, is the traditional festive dish.

Serves 4–6

450g/1lb/2 cups finely minced (ground) lean lamb

1 onion, grated

10ml/2 tsp ground cinnamon

5ml/1 tsp ground cumin

5ml/1 tsp ground allspice

115g/4oz/²/₃ cup fine bulgur, well rinsed and drained

30ml/2 tbsp olive oil, or melted ghee

sea salt and ground black pepper

For the topping

30–45ml/2–3 tbsp olive oil

2–3 onions, halved and sliced with the grain

30–45ml/2–3 tbsp pine nuts

5ml/1 tsp ground cinnamon

15ml/1 tbsp pomegranate molasses

sea salt and ground black pepper

15–30ml/1–2 tbsp light tahini and small bunch of fresh parsley, finely chopped, to serve

Baked kibbeh with onions and pine nuts
Kibbeh saniyeh

There are numerous versions of kibbeh, which is one of Lebanon's treasured national dishes. Here, the kibbeh mixture is baked and topped with onions and pine nuts. In Turkey a similar dish is prepared by Armenians, who top it with a tomato sauce.

1 Preheat the oven to 180°C/350°F/Gas 4 and grease a shallow ovenproof dish, such as a gratin dish or small roasting pan.

2 In a bowl, use a wooden spoon or your fists to pound the lamb with the onion and spices. Season with plenty of salt and pepper and knead well.

3 Add the bulgur to the lamb, and knead again for about 10 minutes, until the mixture is thoroughly mixed and has a paste-like consistency. Alternatively, you can place the mixture in a blender or food processor and whizz to a paste.

4 Turn the mixture into the greased dish and spread it evenly. Flatten the top with your knuckles and spread the oil or ghee over the surface. Using a sharp knife, cut the mixture into wedges or diamond shapes and bake in the oven for about 30 minutes, until nicely browned.

5 Meanwhile, make the topping. Heat the oil in a frying pan and cook the onions until they begin to brown. Add the pine nuts and stir until they turn golden. Add the cinnamon and pomegranate molasses and season with salt and pepper.

6 When the kibbeh is ready, spread the onion mixture over the top and return it to the oven for 5 minutes. Lift the portions on to a serving plate and drizzle the tahini over each one. Garnish with the parsley and serve while still warm.

Energy 399kcal/1659kJ; Protein 20.6g; Carbohydrate 30.4g, of which sugars 9.6g; Fat 22.4g, of which saturates 5.4g; Cholesterol 57mg; Calcium 69mg; Fibre 2.5g; Sodium 73mg

Above: A shrine in the Kannoubin Valley, also known as the Holy Valley.

Serves 4–6

1kg/2¼lb potatoes, scrubbed and halved

300ml/½ pint/1¼ cups milk

100g/3¾oz butter

pinch of freshly grated nutmeg

30ml/2 tbsp olive oil

2 onions, finely chopped

15–30ml/1–2 tbsp pine nuts

5–10ml/1–2 tsp ground cinnamon

5ml/1 tsp ground allspice

450g/1lb/2 cups lean minced (ground) lamb

30ml/2 tbsp white breadcrumbs

30ml/2 tbsp finely grated Parmesan

sea salt and ground black pepper

Cook's tip Depending on variety, the potatoes may absorb more butter and milk: add enough to make the mash taste creamy and light. The pie can be assembled in advance if convenient, ready for baking.

Baked lamb and potato pie
Kaleb batata

This warm, nourishing dish is prepared in homes throughout Lebanon. Enjoyed by the young and the elderly, it is in essence a glorified shepherd's pie, although the meat filling is sandwiched between two layers of potato. It can be prepared with lamb or beef and is delicious served with a salad.

1 Preheat the oven to 180°C/350°F/Gas 4. Place the potatoes in a deep pan and cover with plenty of water. Bring the water to the boil and cook the potatoes for 15–20 minutes, or until they are tender. Drain and refresh under cold running water and peel off the skins.

2 Return the peeled potatoes to the pan and mash with a potato masher or a fork. Add the milk and butter and beat the mashed potatoes over the heat, until they are light and fluffy. Season to taste with grated nutmeg and salt and pepper, cover the pan and set aside.

3 To prepare the filling, heat the olive oil in a heavy-based pan and cook the onions until they begin to colour. Stir in the pine nuts until they begin to colour then add the cinnamon and allspice. Add the minced lamb and cook for 3–4 minutes. Season to taste with salt and pepper.

4 Lightly grease a baking dish and spread a layer of the potato mixture in the base. Spread the meat filling over the top and sandwich the meat with another layer of potato. Mix together the breadcrumbs and cheese and sprinkle them over the top.

5 Place the dish in the oven and bake for 30–40 minutes, until the top is nicely browned. Serve immediately with a salad or vegetable side dish.

Energy 548kcal/2289kJ; Protein 23.3g; Carbohydrate 39.6g, of which sugars 8.7g; Fat 34.2g, of which saturates 16.1g; Cholesterol 104mg; Calcium 174mg; Fibre 2.8g; Sodium 318mg

Spicy meat dumplings with yogurt
Shish barak

Some cooks say shish barak is of Armenian origin, while others believe it developed from an Anatolian dish during the Ottoman Empire. It is regarded as a classic in Lebanon, where it is served in ordinary homes and classy restaurants alike. You can replace the spices in the recipe with sabaa baharat, the Lebanese spice mix available in Middle Eastern stores.

1 To prepare the filling, heat the oil in a heavy pan and cook the onions and chilli until they begin to brown. Stir in the pine nuts and cook for a minute, then add the cinnamon, allspice and paprika. Add the lamb and fry for 2–3 minutes to brown, and season well. Stir in the pomegranate molasses and cook for a minute, then turn off the heat and leave to cool. Preheat the oven to 180°C/350°F/Gas 4.

2 Place the halved sheets of filo in a stack on a clean surface and keep covered. Brush the first sheet with a little melted butter then spoon some of the filling in a line along one of the long edges, stopping about 1cm/¹/₂in from each end. Roll up the pastry into a long finger, tucking in the edges as you roll, then curl it into a tight coil. Repeat with the remaining filo sheets and filling to make 12 coils.

3 Place the filled coils on a lightly greased baking tray and bake them in the oven for about 15 minutes, until the pastry is light golden but not fully cooked.

4 Meanwhile, beat the rice flour and water mixture into the yogurt, and pour the mixture into a wide heavy pan. Stir over a medium heat until the yogurt is at scalding point, then season with salt and pepper and stir in the oregano.

5 Take the filled pastry coils out of the oven and carefully place them in the yogurt. Cook over a gentle heat for 10 minutes. Sprinkle the mint over the top and serve.

Energy 454kcal/1898kJ; Protein 27.2g; Carbohydrate 33.7g, of which sugars 15.8g; Fat 24.8g, of which saturates 9.3g; Cholesterol 88mg; Calcium 381mg; Fibre 1.4g; Sodium 237mg

Serves 6

6 sheets of filo pastry, cut in half

30ml/2 tbsp butter, melted

5ml/1 tsp rice flour or cornflour (cornstarch), slaked with 10ml/2 tsp water

1 litre/1³/₄ pints/4 cups strained yogurt

5ml/1 tsp dried oregano

5ml/1 tsp dried mint

sea salt and ground black pepper

For the filling

30ml/2 tbsp olive oil

2 onions, finely chopped

1 red chilli, seeded and finely chopped

30ml/2 tbsp pine nuts

10ml/2 tsp ground cinnamon

5ml/1 tsp ground allspice

5ml/1 tsp paprika

450g/1lb/2 cups lean minced (ground) lamb

15ml/1 tbsp pomegranate molasses

sea salt and ground black pepper

Serves 4

For the meatballs

450g/1lb/2 cups lean minced
(ground) lamb

5–10ml/1–2 tsp ground cinnamon

5ml/1 tsp ground allspice

sunflower oil, for frying

plain (all-purpose) flour, for coating

sea salt and ground black pepper

1 lemon, cut into wedges, to serve

cooked rice, to accompany

For the sauce

15ml/1 tbsp ghee, or 15ml/1 tbsp olive
oil with a knob of butter

2 onions, halved lengthways, cut in half
crossways, and slice with the grain

30ml/2 tbsp pine nuts

5ml/1 tsp ground cinnamon

400g/14oz can chopped tomatoes

10ml/2 tsp sugar

sea salt and ground black pepper

Pasha's meatballs in tomato sauce
Dawood Pasha

This famous dish of meatballs cooked in a tomato sauce and served with rice is said to have been one of the favourite dishes of Dawood Pasha, the first governor of Mount Lebanon appointed by the Ottomans in 1860. The traditional recipe calls for the meat to be cooked in sheep's tail fat, but ghee, or olive oil with a knob of butter, is a practical substitute.

1 In a bowl, mix together the minced lamb, cinnamon and allspice and season with about 2.5ml/½ tsp salt and a good grinding of black pepper. Knead the mixture well with your hands then, with wet hands, mould it into small balls about the size of large cherries.

2 Heat enough sunflower oil for frying in a heavy pan. Roll the meatballs in a little flour and drop them into the oil. Fry for 4–5 minutes, turning, until they are nicely browned all over. Lift the meatballs out of the oil with a slotted spoon and drain them on kitchen paper.

3 To make the sauce, heat the ghee or olive oil and butter in a heavy pan and sauté the onion over a medium heat for 3–4 minutes, until golden brown. Stir in the pine nuts and cook until they begin to colour, then add the cinnamon, followed by the tomatoes and sugar.

4 Simmer the sauce, uncovered, for about 20 minutes, until it has reduced and thickened, and season with salt and pepper.

5 Place the meatballs in the sauce and heat through for 10 minutes. Serve hot with rice and lemon wedges.

Energy 485kcal/2014kJ; Protein 25.4g; Carbohydrate 18.1g, of which sugars 11.7g; Fat 35.2g, of which saturates 10.9g; Cholesterol 95mg; Calcium 66mg; Fibre 2.7g; Sodium 119mg

Serves 4–6

30ml/2 tbsp ghee, or 30ml/2 tbsp olive oil with a knob of butter

2 onions, finely chopped

2–3 cloves garlic, finely chopped

5ml/1 tsp cumin seeds

5ml/1 tsp coriander seeds

500g/1¼lb lean lamb, cut into cubes

plain (all-purpose) flour, for coating

400ml/14fl oz/1⅔ cups chicken stock

350g/12oz plums, stoned (pitted) and quartered

sea salt and ground black pepper

small bunch of fresh mint leaves, finely shredded, to garnish

plain pilaff, to serve

Lamb stew with plums
Yakhnit al-khawkh

A number of medieval dishes incorporating meat and fruit are still popular in the eastern Mediterranean. The most common include lamb or chicken stewed with apricots, prunes, quinces and plums. They are usually served with a buttery pilaff that may contain a hint of saffron or herbs.

1 Heat the ghee in a heavy pan and cook the onions until they begin to colour, then add the garlic, cumin and coriander seeds.

2 Toss the pieces of lamb in flour to coat them lightly, then add them to the pan to brown. Pour in the stock and bring it to the boil, reduce the heat, cover the pan and simmer for about 40 minutes.

3 Add the plums to the stew and season with salt and pepper. Cover the pan again and simmer for a further 20 minutes, until the plums are tender.

4 Transfer the stew to a warmed serving dish, garnish with the shredded mint, and serve with a plain, buttery pilaff.

Energy 262kcal/1092kJ; Protein 18.4g; Carbohydrate 14.3g, of which sugars 9.6g; Fat 15g, of which saturates 6.7g; Cholesterol 63mg; Calcium 44mg; Fibre 2.1g; Sodium 212mg

Dervish's beads
Masbahat al-derwich

During the Ottoman period, dervish lodges were founded throughout the eastern Mediterranean, resulting in the spread of dishes attributed to the order. Traditionally, the components of this dish are cooked separately then assembled in layers, representing prayers, at the end, but modern cooks opt for the simpler method of cooking all the layers together.

1 Preheat the oven to 180°C/350°F/Gas 4. Heat 30ml/2 tbsp of the oil in a heavy pan and fry the onions until golden brown. Drain on kitchen paper.

2 Lightly butter an ovenproof dish and spread a layer of potatoes over the base. Lay the slices of lamb fillet on top, then the onions, followed by a layer of aubergine, a layer of peppers, and a final layer of tomatoes.

3 Mix the remaining olive oil with the tomato purée, 150ml/¼ pint/⅔ cup water, oregano and plenty of salt and pepper and pour it over the dish. Dot the tomatoes with butter and sprinkle with the sugar and cinnamon. Cover with foil and bake for 45 minutes, then remove the foil and return the dish to the oven for a further 15–20 minutes, until nicely browned. Serve hot with yogurt and a salad.

Energy 365kcal/1527kJ; Protein 18.7g; Carbohydrate 27.7g, of which sugars 13.2g; Fat 20.8g, of which saturates 6.8g; Cholesterol 63mg; Calcium 45mg; Fibre 4.2g; Sodium 111mg

Serves 4–6

60–75ml/4–5 tbsp olive oil

12–15 pearl (baby) onions, peeled

15ml/1 tbsp butter

5–6 potatoes, boiled and sliced

450g/1lb lean lamb fillet, thinly sliced

1 aubergine (eggplant), thinly sliced

1 green and 1 red (bell) pepper, thinly sliced

5–6 tomatoes, thinly sliced

15ml/1 tbsp tomato purée (paste)

5–10ml/1–2 tsp oregano

10ml/2 tsp cane sugar

5–10ml/1–2 tsp ground cinnamon

sea salt and ground black pepper

Roasted leg of lamb with rice
Kharouf mahshi

A simple roasted leg of lamb served on a bed of rice with pine nuts is a classic dish enjoyed throughout the Middle East. Traditionally, a joint of lamb would often be cooked in this way in the communal village oven.

1 Preheat the oven to 200°C/400°F/Gas 6. Rub the lamb with salt and pepper and place it in a roasting pan. Arrange the vegetables and garlic around the lamb and drizzle the oil over them all. Pour in about 300ml/½ pint/1¼ cups water, cover with foil and place the dish in the oven for about 50 minutes.

2 Meanwhile, prepare the rice. Heat the olive oil with the butter in a heavy pan and cook the onions until they begin to colour. Stir in the pine nuts and cook until they begin to colour, then add the cinnamon and the minced lamb. Cook over a medium heat for 2–3 minutes, then stir in the rice, coating the grains in the oil.

3 Add about 500ml/17fl oz/generous 2 cups water to the pan, season with a little salt and pepper, and bring to the boil. Reduce the heat and simmer for 15 minutes, until all the water has been absorbed. Turn off the heat, cover with a clean dish towel, followed by the lid, and leave the rice to steam for 10–15 minutes.

4 Take the lamb out of the oven and remove the foil. Baste, then return to the oven, uncovered, for a further 15 minutes. Remove from the oven, and leave to rest.

5 Sieve (strain) the vegetables and juices, or whizz in a blender or food processor with a dash of wine, to make the gravy. Reheat and transfer to a jug (pitcher).

6 Spoon some of the rice on to a serving dish to make a bed for the lamb. Place the lamb on top of the rice and spoon the rest of the rice around it. Carve and serve immediately with the gravy.

Energy 555kcal/2312kJ; Protein 33.1g; Carbohydrate 39.6g, of which sugars 4.9g; Fat 26.8g, of which saturates 8.9g; Cholesterol 115mg; Calcium 36mg; Fibre 1.3g; Sodium 113mg

Above: Wild lavender growing on the road from the Bekaa Valley to Mount Lebanon.

Serves 6

1kg/2¼lb leg of lamb

2 carrots, peeled and chopped

1 red (bell) pepper, chopped

6 cloves garlic, peeled and lightly crushed

30–45ml/2–3 tbsp olive oil

a little red wine

sea salt and ground black pepper

For the rice

15ml/1 tbsp olive oil plus a knob of butter

1 onion, finely chopped

30ml/2 tbsp pine nuts

10ml/2 tsp ground cinnamon

100g/3¾oz/½ cup lean minced (ground) lamb

250g/9oz/1¼ cups long grain rice, well rinsed and drained

Cook's tip If you prefer, pierce the lamb in places with the point of a sharp knife and insert the garlic in slivers instead of cooking it with the other vegetables around the joint.

Serves 4–6

2–3 large onions

250g/9oz/generous 1 cup lean minced (ground) lamb

90g/3¹/₂oz/¹/₂ cup long grain rice, rinsed and drained

15ml/1 tbsp tomato paste (purée)

10ml/2 tsp ground cinnamon

5ml/1 tsp ground allspice

5ml/1 tsp ground cumin

5ml/1 tsp ground coriander

small bunch of fresh parsley, finely chopped

30–45ml/2–3 tbsp olive oil

15–30ml/1–2 tbsp white wine or cider vinegar

5–10ml/1–2 tsp sugar

15ml/1 tbsp butter

sea salt and ground black pepper

1 lemon, cut into wedges, to serve

Cook's tip The Lebanese spice mix, sabaa baharat, a combination of pepper, cinnamon, coriander, cumin, paprika, cloves and nutmeg, is often used in this dish.

Roasted onions stuffed with lamb
Mahshi basal

Lebanese markets display a variety of onions: some for salads or pickles, others for stews and kebabs, and yet others that are ideal for stripping into layers and stuffing, as in this recipe. Large golden or red onions are suitable for this dish, which can be served as an appetizer, as an accompaniment to grilled or roasted meats, or on its own with a salad.

1 Bring a pan of water to the boil. Make a cut down one side of each onion, cutting into the centre from top to bottom. Cook the onions in the boiling water for about 10 minutes, until they soften and the layers begin to separate. Drain and refresh the onions under cold running water and carefully detach the layers.

2 In a bowl, pound the meat thoroughly with your hands. Add the rice, tomato purée, spices, parsley (reserving a little) and seasoning and knead well to mix.

3 Spread out the onion layers and place a spoonful of the meat mixture in each one. Roll them up loosely, leaving room for the rice to expand as it cooks, and tuck in any open ends.

4 Preheat the oven to 200°C/400°F/Gas 6. Pack the stuffed onion layers close together in a heavy pan and pour over the olive oil, vinegar and sugar. Cover and cook the onions over a medium heat for about 25 minutes, until the meat and rice are cooked.

5 Dot the stuffed onions with a little butter and place in the oven, uncovered, for 15–20 minutes, until they are nicely browned on top and slightly caramelized. Garnish with the reserved parsley and serve hot with wedges of lemon.

Energy 263kcal/1094kJ; Protein 12.2g; Carbohydrate 29g, of which sugars 11.4g; Fat 11.4g, of which saturates 4.1g; Cholesterol 37mg; Calcium 59mg; Fibre 2.4g; Sodium 67mg

Stuffed artichoke bottoms
Ardishawk bil lahma

When globe artichokes are in season, you will find this dish being prepared in homes throughout the eastern Mediterranean region. Tasty and impressive looking, it is quite time-consuming to prepare if using fresh artichokes, but you can make life a lot easier by buying frozen artichoke bottoms, which are available in Middle Eastern stores and some supermarkets.

1 Preheat the oven to 180°C/350°F/Gas 4. Heat the oil in a heavy pan and cook the onions for 2–3 minutes until they begin to colour.

2 Stir in the pine nuts, reserving a few for garnishing, and cook for 1–2 minutes until they turn golden, then add the lamb and spices and fry until the lamb begins to brown. Season with salt and pepper.

3 Place the artichoke bottoms, side by side, in a shallow ovenproof dish. Using a spoon, fill the artichokes with the meat mixture.

4 Combine the lemon juice and water in a bowl and stir in the flour, making sure it is thoroughly blended, then pour the mixture over the artichokes.

5 Cover the dish with foil and place it in the oven for 25–30 minutes, until the artichokes are tender. Meanwhile, heat a frying pan and dry roast the reserved pine nuts until golden brown.

6 Remove the stuffed artichokes from the oven and transfer to a warmed serving dish. Sprinkle the roasted pine nuts over the top of the artichokes and serve with wedges of lemon to squeeze over them.

Serves 4

30ml/2 tbsp olive oil

2 medium onions, finely chopped

15–30ml/1–2 tbsp pine nuts

350g/12oz/1½ cups lean minced (ground) lamb

5ml/1 tsp ground cinnamon

2.5ml/½ tsp ground allspice

4–6 fresh or frozen artichoke bottoms

juice of 1 lemon

200ml/7fl oz/scant 1 cup water

15ml/1 tbsp plain (all-purpose) flour

sea salt and ground black pepper

1 lemon, cut into wedges, to serve

Energy 277kcal/1153kJ; Protein 19.7g; Carbohydrate 14.3g, of which sugars 7.3g; Fat 16.1g, of which saturates 5.4g; Cholesterol 67mg; Calcium 61mg; Fibre 2.2g; Sodium 96mg

Cook's tip Fresh artichokes should be treated like flowers and kept with their stems in water until ready to use. To prepare them for this dish, pull off the outer leaves, cut off the stalks and slice away the purple choke, the small leaves and any hard bits. Remove any fibres with the edge of a spoon and rub the artichoke bottoms with a mixture of lemon juice and salt to prevent them from discolouring.

Serves 4–6

450g/1lb lean boneless lamb, cut into bitesize chunks

about 12 small shallots or pearl (baby) onions, peeled and left whole

about 8 cloves garlic, peeled

2 cinnamon sticks

5ml/1 tsp fennel seeds

5ml/1 tsp cumin seeds

6 peppercorns

45–60ml/3–4 tbsp white wine or cider vinegar

2 courgettes (zucchini), cut into bitesize chunks

2 medium aubergines (eggplants), cut into bitesize chunks

10ml/2 tsp dried mint

sea salt

Lamb and vegetable stew
Lahm bi-khal

This traditional dish is reputed to have been a favourite of the Prophet Muhammad. The vinegar acts as a preservative, enabling the dish to last for a number of days. It is fairly delicate and is generally eaten with chunks of bread to mop up the juices.

1 Place the meat in a deep pan with the shallots, garlic, cinnamon, fennel and cumin seeds and the peppercorns. Add water to cover and bring to the boil, skimming off any foam. Reduce the heat, cover and simmer for 35–40 minutes, until the meat is tender.

2 Season with salt and stir in the vinegar. Add the courgettes and aubergines and bring the liquid back to the boil. Reduce the heat, cover the pan and simmer for a further 10 minutes, until the vegetables are cooked but not mushy. Transfer the stew to a serving dish, sprinkle the mint over the top and serve immediately.

Energy 182kcal/758kJ; Protein 17.5g; Carbohydrate 7.5g, of which sugars 5.3g; Fat 9.4g, of which saturates 4.1g; Cholesterol 57mg; Calcium 46mg; Fibre 2.6g; Sodium 69mg

Aromatic chicken on toasted pitta bread
Shawarma dajaj

The shawarma dishes of Lebanon are the equivalent of the Turkish döner kebab and are popular street food. When made with chicken, it is marinated first in a deliciously aromatic combination of spices and served in pitta bread with a tahini sauce, tomatoes and pickles. At home, you can bake the chicken in the oven or cook it under a grill.

1 Mix together the ingredients for the marinade and toss the chicken breasts in the mixture, then cover and leave in the refrigerator to marinate for at least 6 hours.

2 Preheat the oven to 180°C/350°F/Gas 4. Lay the chicken in an ovenproof dish, baste it with the marinade, and place it in the oven for about 20 minutes.

3 Lift out the chicken and slice it finely, then return it to the dish. Baste with the cooking juices, season with salt, and return to the oven for a further 10 minutes.

4 Place the pitta breads on an oven tray and toast them in the oven for 5 minutes. Serve the chicken in the pitta pouches, or on top of the pitta bread, and accompany it with a tahini sauce and pickled vegetables.

Energy 408kcal/1726kJ; Protein 40.2g; Carbohydrate 44.7g, of which sugars 1.8g; Fat 8.9g, of which saturates 2.1g; Cholesterol 65mg; Calcium 90mg; Fibre 1.7g; Sodium 499mg

Serves 4

4 chicken breasts

sea salt

4 pitta breads

tahini sauce and pickled vegetables, to serve

For the marinade

30–45ml/2–3 tbsp olive oil

juice of 2–3 lemons

10ml/2 tsp white wine or cider vinegar

2 cloves garlic, crushed

1 cinnamon stick, broken into pieces

grated rind of $1/2$ orange

4–6 cardamom pods, crushed

ground black pepper

Roasted stuffed turkey with thyme
Habash mahshi

Among the Christian communities of Lebanon, turkey is the traditional centrepiece for the Christmas meal. Around this time, live turkeys are shepherded through the markets and busy neighbourhoods, reminding cooks to begin their preparations.

1 Preheat the oven to 200°C/400°F/Gas 6. To make the stuffing, heat the oil with the butter in a heavy pan and cook the onions until they begin to colour. Add the pine nuts, almonds and currants and stir until the nuts begin to brown and the currants plump up. Add the lamb and cinnamon and stir until browned.

2 Stir in the rice, coating it with the oil, and pour in the chicken stock. Season with salt and pepper and bring to the boil. Reduce the heat and simmer gently for about 15 minutes, until the liquid has been absorbed. Remove from the heat.

3 Season the turkey inside and out with salt and pepper. Stuff the cavity with the rice mixture and secure the opening with a skewer. Rub the turkey with butter and place it breast side up in a roasting pan. Arrange half the sprigs of thyme around the turkey and roast for about 30 minutes.

4 Reduce the heat to 180°C/350°F/Gas 4. Baste the turkey with the cooking juices and pour about 250ml/8fl oz/1 cup water into the dish. Roast for a further 1½–2 hours, or until the juices run clear when the thigh is pierced with a skewer.

5 Transfer the turkey to a serving platter and garnish with fresh sprigs of thyme. Cover with foil to keep it warm and leave it to rest for 15 minutes before carving. Reduce the cooking juices over a medium heat, skimming off the fat, and season to taste. Pour the juices into a jug (pitcher) and serve with the turkey.

Serves 4–6

1 medium turkey, approximately 2.25–2.5kg/5–5½lb

115g/4oz/1½ cup butter, softened

6–8 sprigs of fresh thyme

sea salt and ground black pepper

For the stuffing

30ml/2 tbsp olive oil plus a knob of butter

2 onions, finely chopped

30ml/2 tbsp pine nuts

30ml/2 tbsp blanched almonds, chopped

30ml/2 tbsp currants

225g/8oz/1 cup lean minced (ground) lamb

10–15ml/2–3 tsp ground cinnamon

250g/9oz/1¼ cups short grain rice

500ml/17fl oz/generous 2 cups chicken stock

sea salt and ground black pepper

Energy 761kcal/3174kJ; Protein 63.9g; Carbohydrate 43.4g, of which sugars 7.6g; Fat 36.9g, of which saturates 12.5g; Cholesterol 235mg; Calcium 68mg; Fibre 1.5g; Sodium 272mg

VEGETABLE DISHES & PRESERVES

Spicy potatoes with coriander

Chicory in olive oil

Stuffed aubergines in oil

Roasted courgettes with vinegar

Baked courgettes with cheese

Spinach with yogurt

Baked vegetable stew

Jerusalem artichoke and tomato stew

Baked red cabbage with quince and walnuts

Apricots stuffed with rice

Pickled white cabbage with walnuts

Pickled stuffed aubergines

Ornaments of the dining table

Vegetables have featured in the cooking of the eastern Mediterranean since ancient times, but attained glory in the medieval period, which was greatly influenced by the cuisine of Persia. Numerous dishes were dedicated to vegetables alone, and they were held in such high esteem that they became the focus of Arab sayings: 'Vegetables are the ornaments of the dining table,' or, 'A table without vegetables is like an old man devoid of wisdom.' The Ottomans introduced vegetables from the New World through their trading alliance with Spain, including corn, potatoes, bell peppers and, most importantly, tomatoes and chillies – two key ingredients in the cooking of the region.

The Fertile Crescent was not given its name for nothing – its rich soil and climate suit grain and vegetables, and the markets offer seasonal vegetables in great abundance and variety. Vegetables and fruit go hand in hand, as some fruits are cooked and served as vegetables, or are combined with them in stews, while several vegetables, such as aubergine, pumpkin and courgette, are poached with sugar and served as sweets or jam. As meat has always been scarce and expensive, poor people have depended heavily on vegetables, beans and lentils. The most useful of all, the aubergine, was known as 'poor man's meat' but was equally enjoyed at the lavish banquets of caliphs and sultans.

Lebanon and Turkey outrank all the neighbouring countries with their variety of vegetable dishes. Vegetables appear in numerous mezze dishes, pickles, salads, stews, pilaffs, jams and puddings, and Lebanese Christians depend on a range of vegetarian dishes during periods of fasting.

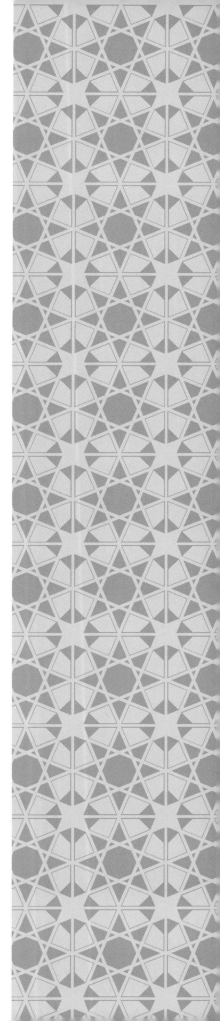

Serves 4

350g/12oz new potatoes

60ml/4 tbsp olive oil or 30ml/2 tbsp ghee

3–4 cloves garlic, finely chopped

2 red chillies, seeded and finely chopped

5–10ml/1–2 tsp cumin seeds

bunch of fresh coriander (cilantro),
finely chopped

sea salt and ground black pepper

1 lemon, cut into wedges, to serve

Cook's tip If the dish is to be eaten at room temperature it is preferable to cook the potatoes in olive oil, but ghee is often used instead when they are to be served hot.

Spicy potatoes with coriander
Batata harra

The spices in this popular potato dish vary across Lebanon, Syria and Jordan but the recipes invariably include chillies and cumin. The dish can be eaten at room temperature as part of a mezze spread, but is also often served hot as an accompaniment to grilled and roasted meat and fish.

1 Steam the potatoes with their skins on for about 10 minutes, until they are cooked but still firm. Drain them and refresh under cold running water. Peel off the skins and cut the potatoes into bitesize pieces.

2 Heat the oil or ghee in a heavy pan and cook the garlic, chillies and cumin seeds for 2–3 minutes, until they begin to colour. Add the potatoes, turning them to make sure they are coated in the oil and spices, and fry for about 5 minutes.

3 Season the potatoes with salt and pepper and stir in most of the coriander. (If serving the dish at room temperature, leave the potatoes to cool first.) Sprinkle the remaining coriander over the top and serve the potatoes from the pan with lemon wedges to squeeze over them.

Energy 174kcal/723kJ; Protein 2.4g; Carbohydrate 15.5g, of which sugars 1.2g; Fat 11.8g, of which saturates 1.7g; Cholesterol 0mg; Calcium 16mg; Fibre 0.9g; Sodium 12mg

Chicory in olive oil
Asoura

Chicory is a popular vegetable in Lebanon. In other parts of the Middle East, this dish is known as hindbeh bi-zeit, literally 'chicory with olive oil', but the Lebanese call it asoura, meaning 'squeezed', as the cooked chicory is squeezed by hand to get rid of all excess water. It is served as a mezze dish or as an accompaniment to meat, poultry or fish.

1 Bring a pan of water to the boil. Drop in the chicory and boil for 10 minutes, until soft. Drain and refresh under cold running water.

2 Take the chicory in your hands and squeeze tightly to remove all the excess water, so that it is almost dry. Divide it into four portions and squeeze them into tight balls. Cover and leave in the refrigerator until ready to serve.

3 Just before serving, place each ball on a plate and flatten it out with the palm of your hand, or the back of a wooden spoon. Drizzle each one with olive oil and a little lemon juice and sprinkle with salt and pepper.

Energy 109kcal/447kJ; Protein 0.5g; Carbohydrate 2.5g, of which sugars 0.7g; Fat 11.5g, of which saturates 1.7g; Cholesterol 0mg; Calcium 19mg; Fibre 0.8g; Sodium 1mg

Serves 4

about 350g/12oz chicory

45ml/3 tbsp olive oil

juice of 1 lemon

sea salt and ground black pepper

Above: Some of the restored buildings and mosque in the centre of the city of Beirut.

Serves 4–6

150ml/¼ pint/⅔ cup olive oil

1 onion, finely chopped

2 tomatoes, skinned, seeded and chopped

10ml/2 tsp sabaa baharat

10ml/2 tsp dried mint

5–10ml/1–2 tsp sugar

175g/6oz/¾ cup short grain rice

6 medium slim aubergines (eggplants)

1–2 small potatoes, sliced

juice of 1 lemon

sea salt and ground black pepper

Cook's tips For this recipe, most of the aubergine flesh is removed and it is not added to the filling. It is generally discarded but could be used in another dish.

The stuffed aubergines need to stand up while cooking, so that they are surrounded by the cooking liquid but not submerged in it, so choose a pan into which they will fit fairly snugly, standing side by side.

Stuffed aubergines in oil
Batinjan bi zeit

There are many variations of stuffed vegetable dishes throughout the eastern Mediterranean region. In Lebanon, the local spice mix, sabaa baharat, which is a blend of seven spices, is often used to flavour the rice filling in this dish, but if you cannot find it you can just use a combination of ground cumin, coriander and cinnamon. Serve these stuffed aubergines as an accompaniment to any roast fish or meat, or on their own as an appetizer.

1 To make the stuffing, heat 15ml/1 tbsp of the olive oil in a heavy pan and cook the onion for 2–3 minutes until it begins to colour. Add the tomatoes, spice mix, mint and a little sugar and cook for 2–3 minutes.

2 Add the rice to the pan, coating it well in the oil, and pour in enough water to cover the rice by a finger's width. Season with salt and pepper and bring to the boil. Reduce the heat and simmer for 10 minutes, until all the water has been absorbed. Turn off the heat, cover the pan with a clean dish towel and put on the lid. Leave the rice to steam for 10 minutes.

3 Meanwhile, prepare the aubergines. Cut off the stalks and use an apple corer to hollow out the middle, or pummel the aubergines with your fingers to loosen the flesh from the skin and squeeze out the flesh through the opening at the stalk end.

4 Fill each aubergine with the rice mixture and seal the opening with a slice of potato. Stand the aubergines in a heavy pan.

5 Mix the lemon juice and remaining olive oil with 100ml/3½fl oz/scant ½ cup water and pour it around the aubergines. Bring to the boil, reduce the heat, cover the pan and simmer for about 40 minutes. Serve hot or at room temperature.

Energy 486kcal/2023kJ; Protein 10.8g; Carbohydrate 76.2g, of which sugars 34.9g; Fat 16.8g, of which saturates 2.3g; Cholesterol 0mg; Calcium 160mg; Fibre 10.8g; Sodium 26mg

Roasted courgettes with vinegar
Koussa bil khal

The courgette is a very popular vegetable in the eastern Mediterranean region, and in the markets you can find marbled green courgettes and white ones as well as the more usual green type. Any kind will do for this recipe, which makes a lovely side dish for grilled or roasted meats and fish.

1 Preheat the oven to 180°C/350°F/Gas 4. Place the courgette slices in an ovenproof dish with the garlic cloves.

2 Pour the olive oil over the courgettes, and roast in the oven for 25–30 minutes, until softened and lightly browned.

3 Lift the courgette slices and some of the garlic out of the dish and arrange on a warmed serving plate. Mix 30–45ml/2–3 tbsp of the cooking oil with the vinegar and dried mint and drizzle it over the courgettes. Sprinkle with salt and serve warm or at room temperature.

Energy 78kcal/322kJ; Protein 2.7g; Carbohydrate 3.3g, of which sugars 2.1g; Fat 6g, of which saturates 0.9g; Cholesterol 0mg; Calcium 36mg; Fibre 1.3g; Sodium 2mg

Serves 4–6

4–6 courgettes (zucchini), trimmed and sliced lengthways

4 cloves garlic, halved and lightly crushed

45–60ml/3–4 tbsp olive oil

30ml/2 tbsp cider or white wine vinegar

10ml/2 tsp dried mint

sea salt

Serves 4–6

30ml/2 tbsp olive oil plus a knob
of butter

2 onions, cut in half lengthways and
sliced finely with the grain

5–10ml/1–2 tsp caraway seeds

4–6 firm courgettes (zucchini), trimmed
and cut into thick slices lengthways

4 eggs

250g/9oz feta or Parmesan cheese,
crumbled or grated

2.5ml/½ tsp paprika

sea salt and ground black pepper

Baked courgettes with cheese
Kousa bi gebna

This is a popular supper dish throughout the eastern Mediterranean. It
makes a good light meal eaten with yogurt and bread, but is also an ideal
accompaniment to roast meat. A tangy cheese made of ewe's milk, such as
feta, is usually used for this recipe, but you can also use Parmesan.

1 Preheat the oven to 180°C/350°F/Gas 4. Heat the oil with the butter in a heavy
pan. Stir in the onions and cook until soft and just beginning to colour. Toss in the
caraway seeds and turn off the heat.

2 Place the courgette slices in a steamer and steam for about 10 minutes until
tender but not mushy. Drain well and spread half the slices in the base of an
ovenproof dish. Spread the onion mixture, including the oil and butter, over the top
and arrange another layer of courgettes over the onions.

3 Beat the eggs, then mix in the cheese and paprika. Season generously with salt
and pepper and pour the egg mixture over the courgettes. Bake the dish for
20–25 minutes, until the top is golden brown. Serve immediately.

Energy 314kcal/1302kJ; Protein 23.3g; Carbohydrate 7.2g, of which sugars 5.4g; Fat 21.6g, of which
saturates 10.2g; Cholesterol 169mg; Calcium 562mg; Fibre 1.8g; Sodium 504mg

Spinach with yogurt
Fattet al sabanekh

Popular throughout the Lebanon, Jordan and Syria, this dish is delicious served on its own or as accompaniment to meatballs (kafta). As with all traditional fatta dishes, which were probably devised as a way of using up stale bread, the spinach is served on toasted flat bread and topped with melted butter and pine nuts.

1 To prepare the yogurt sauce, beat the yogurt with the garlic, tahini and lemon juice and season it to taste with salt and pepper. Set aside.

2 Put the spinach in a steamer or a large pan and cook briefly until just wilted. Refresh under cold running water, drain and squeeze out the excess water. Chop the spinach coarsely.

3 Heat the oil in a heavy pan, stir in the onion and cook for 2–3 minutes. Stir in the spices and then add the spinach, making sure all the leaves are thoroughly mixed with the spiced oil. Cook for a further 2–3 minutes, until the spinach is wilted. Season well with salt and pepper. Mix in the coriander and flaked almonds.

4 Break the toasted pitta bread into bitesize pieces and arrange them in a serving dish. Spread the spinach over the top of the bread and spoon the yogurt sauce over the spinach.

5 Quickly melt the butter in a frying pan and add the pine nuts. Stir fry until the pine nuts are golden in colour. Drizzle the butter from the pan over the yogurt and sprinkle the pine nuts on top. Serve immediately while the spinach is still warm.

Energy 435kcal/1818kJ; Protein 19.3g; Carbohydrate 45.1g, of which sugars 20g; Fat 21.3g, of which saturates 4.8g; Cholesterol 11mg; Calcium 625mg; Fibre 5.9g; Sodium 529mg

Above: One of the ancient olive trees still producing fruit in Lebanon.

Serves 4

500g/1¼lb fresh spinach, washed and drained

15–30ml/1–2 tbsp olive oil

1 onion, chopped

5ml/1 tsp ground cinnamon

5ml/1 tsp paprika

5ml/1 tsp ground cumin

small bunch of fresh coriander (cilantro), finely chopped

15–30ml/1–2 tbsp flaked (sliced) almonds

2 pitta breads, toasted

15ml/1 tbsp butter

15–30ml/1–2 tbsp pine nuts

sea salt and ground black pepper

For the yogurt sauce

600ml/1 pint/2½ cups creamy, strained yogurt

2 cloves garlic, crushed

30ml/2 tbsp tahini

juice of ½ lemon

sea salt and ground black pepper

Baked vegetable stew
Khudra bil furn

In various parts of the Middle East vegetables are often baked or stewed with cuts of lamb to provide a hearty meal in one dish. However, when they are prepared as mezze, or as accompaniment to a meat dish, the meat is generally omitted. Any seasonal vegetable can be prepared in this manner, but the most popular combination in the eastern Mediterranean includes a mixture of courgettes, tomatoes and peppers.

1 Preheat the oven to 200°C/400°F/Gas 6 and lightly grease a baking dish with a little of the olive oil.

2 Thinly slice the tomatoes and line the base of the prepared baking dish with half the slices. Finely slice the potatoes and arrange in a layer on top of the tomatoes, followed by a layer of thinly sliced courgettes.

3 Cut the onions in half lengthways, and slice with the grain, and thinly slice the peppers. Toss the onion and pepper slices together with the chopped parsley and mint, then sprinkle the mixture over the courgettes. Complete the layering with the rest of the tomato slices.

4 Combine the rest of the olive oil with the lemon juice, garlic and sugar. Season with salt and pepper and pour the mixture over the vegetables.

5 Cover the dish with foil and bake in the oven for about 40 minutes, then remove the foil, dot the butter over the tomatoes and return the dish to the oven to cook, uncovered, for a further 15–20 minutes.

6 Serve the baked vegetables immediately, with yogurt and flat bread or as an accompaniment to a meat or poultry dish.

Energy 306kcal/1280kJ; Protein 7.4g; Carbohydrate 42.7g, of which sugars 16.2g; Fat 12.8g, of which saturates 2g; Cholesterol 0mg; Calcium 101mg; Fibre 6.3g; Sodium 37mg

Serves 6

150ml/¼ pint/⅔ cup olive oil

6 large tomatoes

4–6 potatoes, peeled

3 courgettes (zucchini)

2 onions

2 (bell) peppers

small bunch parsley, finely chopped

bunch fresh mint, finely chopped

juice of 1 lemon

2 cloves garlic, crushed

10ml/2 tsp sugar

sea salt and ground black pepper

Serves 4

30–45ml/2–3 tbsp olive oil

2 onions, finely chopped

2 cloves garlic, finely chopped

500g/1¼lb Jerusalem artichokes, peeled and cut into bitesize pieces

2 x 400g/14oz cans chopped tomatoes

10–15ml/2–3 tsp sugar

sea salt and ground black pepper

small bunch of fresh coriander (cilantro), finely chopped, to garnish

1 lemon, cut into wedges, to serve

Jerusalem artichoke and tomato stew
Tartoufa

Almost any vegetable is cooked with tomatoes in the Middle East. The garlicky tomato sauce can be mopped up with bread and the method of cooking results in tender, tasty vegetables. Jerusalem artichokes are excellent cooked this way and can be served on their own or as an accompaniment to grilled or roasted meat and poultry dishes.

1 Heat the oil in a heavy pan, stir in the onions and cook until they begin to colour. Add the garlic and the pieces of artichoke, and toss well to make sure they are coated in the oil.

2 Add the tomatoes with the sugar, cover the pan and cook gently for 25–30 minutes, until the artichokes are tender.

3 Remove the lid and bubble up the sauce over a high heat to reduce it a little. Season with salt and pepper and transfer to a serving dish. Garnish with some coriander and serve with wedges of lemon to squeeze over the dish.

Energy 147kcal/619kJ; Protein 3.6g; Carbohydrate 19.8g, of which sugars 17g; Fat 6.6g, of which saturates 1g; Cholesterol 0mg; Calcium 98mg; Fibre 5.1g; Sodium 97mg

Baked red cabbage with quince and walnuts
Koromb wa safarjal

Originally of Armenian origin, this dish spread throughout the eastern Mediterranean as the Armenians migrated from the Caucasus, taking with them their love of vegetables combined with fruit. Simple to prepare, this delicious dish is best served to accompany roasted lamb, duck or chicken.

1 Preheat the oven to 180°C/350°F/Gas 4. Grease a baking dish and arrange the cabbage in it. Pour half the melted butter over the cabbage and toss with half the cinnamon, salt and pepper, lemon juice and pomegranate molasses. Cover the dish with foil and bake for about 30 minutes.

2 Meanwhile, quarter and core the quinces. Cut them into thin slices and submerge them in a bowl of cold water mixed with a squeeze of lemon juice to prevent them from discolouring.

3 Take the cabbage out of the oven and arrange the quince slices over the top. Sprinkle them with sugar and the remaining cinnamon and sprinkle the walnuts over the top. Pour the rest of the butter over the quinces. Cover the dish and bake for a further 20 minutes, then remove the foil and return the dish to the oven for about 10 minutes to brown the top. Serve immediately.

Energy 224kcal/927kJ; Protein 2.6g; Carbohydrate 13.5g, of which sugars 12.5g; Fat 18g, of which saturates 10.5g; Cholesterol 44mg; Calcium 73mg; Fibre 3.6g; Sodium 155mg

Serves 4–6

1 red cabbage, quartered, cored and chopped into bitesize pieces

115g/4oz/¹/₂ cup butter, melted

5–10ml/1–2 tsp ground cinnamon

juice of 1 lemon

10ml/2 tsp pomegranate molasses

2 quinces

15–30ml/1–2 tbsp sugar

15–30ml/1–2 tbsp walnuts, roughly chopped

sea salt and ground black pepper

Apricots stuffed with rice
Mishmish mahshi

This is one of a number of savoury specialities from the rich medieval legacy of sumptuous dishes cooked with fruit. It can be prepared with a filling of rice mixed with minced lamb, to serve on its own, or without meat for serving as an accompaniment to roasted meat and poultry dishes.

1 Preheat the oven to 180°C/350°F/Gas 4. Heat the oil in a heavy pan, stir in the onion and cook until it begins to colour. Toss in the pine nuts until they turn golden, then stir in the rice, making sure the grains are coated in the oil.

2 Add the spices, sugar, mint and tomato to the pan, season with salt and pepper, and pour in about 350ml/12fl oz/1½ cups water to cover the rice. Bring to the boil, stir once, then reduce the heat and leave the rice to simmer for 10–15 minutes, until all the water has been absorbed, then remove from the heat.

3 Meanwhile, prepare the apricots. Using a sharp knife, slit them in half lengthways, making sure they remain attached at one side. Remove the stone (pit) and, if necessary, scrape away a little of the flesh to make room for the filling.

4 Spoon a portion of the rice mixture into the hollow of each apricot, so that it looks plump and appetizing. Place the apricots upright in a lightly greased, shallow baking dish, packing them tightly together so that they support each other during cooking.

5 Mix together the ingredients for the cooking liquid and pour it over and around the apricots. Cover the dish with foil and bake for about 20 minutes.

6 Remove the foil and baste the apricots with the cooking juices. Dot each one with a little butter and return the dish to the oven to cook, uncovered, for a further 5–10 minutes. Serve immediately.

Serves 4

30ml/2 tbsp olive oil

1 onion, finely chopped

15ml/1 tbsp pine nuts

175g/6oz/¾ cup short grain or pudding rice, well rinsed and drained

5ml/1 tsp ground cinnamon

5ml/1 tsp ground allspice

5ml/1 tsp sugar

5ml/1 tsp dried mint

1 large tomato, skinned, seeded and finely chopped

16 fresh apricots

15ml/1 tbsp butter

sea salt and ground black pepper

For the cooking liquid

120ml/4fl oz/½ cup olive oil

50ml/2fl oz/¼ cup water

juice of 1 lemon

10–15ml/2–3 tsp sugar

5ml/1 tsp pomegranate molasses

Cook's tip To use dried apricots, soak them overnight then poach them in the soaking water for 10–15 minutes. Drain well, and stuff the larger ones. Use the smaller ones for another dish, or chop finely and add to the rice.

Energy 449kcal/1872kJ; Protein 6.8g; Carbohydrate 54.1g, of which sugars 16.3g; Fat 23.3g, of which saturates 4.6g; Cholesterol 9mg; Calcium 57mg; Fibre 3.8g; Sodium 37mg

Pickled white cabbage with walnuts
Malfouf mkhalal

Most cabbages grown in Lebanon are white or light green with firm, tender leaves that impart a natural sweetness to dishes. One of the most popular salads of the region is simply shredded cabbage leaves in lemon juice, a dish that will disappear as quickly as it is made.

1 Steam the cabbage leaves for 5–6 minutes. Refresh under cold water and drain well. Lay the leaves on a flat surface and trim the central ribs, so that they lie flat.

2 Using a mortar and pestle, pound the garlic with a little salt until creamy. Add the walnuts and pound to a gritty paste. Add the chilli and bind the mixture with the oil.

3 Place a spoonful of the mixture near the top of each leaf. Pull the top edge over the mixture, tuck in the sides and roll the leaf into a tight log.

4 Pack the stuffed leaves tightly into a sterilized jar and pour over the vinegar. Seal the jar, and leave the cabbage parcels to marinate for at least a week. After opening, they can be stored in the refrigerator for 4–5 days. Serve as a mezze dish, drizzled in olive oil, or as accompaniment to cheese or grilled meats.

Energy 440kcal/1816kJ; Protein 9.8g; Carbohydrate 7g, of which sugars 6.5g; Fat 41.5g, of which saturates 3.5g; Cholesterol 0mg; Calcium 110mg; Fibre 4.3g; Sodium 12mg

Serves 4

8 large white cabbage leaves, or 16 smaller ones

4 cloves garlic

225g/8oz/2 cups shelled walnuts, coarsely chopped

1 fresh chilli, seeded and finely chopped

15ml/1 tbsp olive oil

300ml/$\frac{1}{2}$ pint/1$\frac{1}{4}$ cups cider or white wine vinegar

sea salt

Serves 4–6

12 baby aubergines (eggplants), round or oblong, with stalks removed

1 leek, cut in half if very long

225g/8oz/2 cups walnuts, finely chopped

1 red (bell) pepper, finely chopped

4 cloves garlic, finely chopped

1 red or green chilli, seeded and finely chopped

5–10ml/1–2 tsp sea salt

15ml/1 tbsp olive oil

small bunch of flat leaf parsley leaves

600ml/1 pint/2¹⁄₂ cups white wine vinegar

Pickled stuffed aubergines
Batinjan makdous

Aubergines come in varying sizes and shapes and are used in numerous savoury dishes and several sweet ones too. Pickled stuffed aubergines are a great favourite, served as a mezze dish or devoured as a snack followed by the pickling liquid to quench the thirst.

1 Bring a pan of water to the boil and drop in the aubergines and the leek. Cook for about 10 minutes to soften, then drain and refresh under cold running water. Leave the aubergines to drain in a colander while you prepare the filling. Cut the leek into long thin strips and set aside.

2 Mix together the walnuts, pepper, garlic, chilli and salt and bind with the olive oil. Using a sharp knife, make a slit in the side of each aubergine and stuff the hollow with the filling. Finish with a few parsley leaves stuffed in at the end and carefully wind a strip of leek around the aubergine to bind it and keep it intact.

3 Pack the bound aubergines tightly into a sterilized jar and pour over the vinegar. Seal and store in a cool place for 2–3 weeks. As long as they are always sealed and topped up with vinegar, these aubergines will keep for several months.

Energy 324kcal/1342kJ; Protein 8.4g; Carbohydrate 8.7g, of which sugars 7.7g; Fat 28.7g, of which saturates 2.6g; Cholesterol 0mg; Calcium 82mg; Fibre 6.9g; Sodium 11mg

SWEET DISHES & DRINKS

Milk pudding with mastic

Spiced ground rice pudding

Cream cheese pudding with syrup and nuts

Sweet turmeric cakes

Semolina cake with poppy seeds

Nights of Lebanon

Puffed fritters in syrup

Wheat in fragrant honey

Pomegranate salad with pine nuts and honey

Stuffed red date preserve

Quince preserve

Lebanese coffee with cardamom

Rose water sherbet

Jewelled fruits, scented cakes and drinks

The sweets of the eastern Mediterranean have been renowned since medieval times, when poems, stories and songs were written about the outstanding confectioners of Aleppo and Baghdad. They included sweetmeats prepared with dried dates and figs, jewelled fruit and almond compotes, sugar-coated roasted chickpeas (mulabbas) and solid blocks of crushed sesame seeds with honey (halwa). During the Ottoman era, the creative chefs of the Topkapı Palace came up with new versions of the medieval sweets, introducing sumptuous milk puddings and sweet pastries such as the sophisticated baklava, which spread throughout the empire.

To this day, the choice is astounding: a tantalizing array of syrupy pastries, cakes, milk puddings, ice creams, poached or candied fruits, almond and pistachio marzipans. Cakes and sweet treats are eaten at any time of day, although some may be served as the conclusion to a meal, such as the milk puddings, flavoured with rose or orange blossom waters, vanilla, mastic, aniseed or cinnamon. These puddings look magnificent as an impressive dessert, but people most often end their meals with fresh fruit instead.

As many of the region's fruits are sweet and juicy in season, they are the perfect way to round off a meal. Fruits such as pomegranates, mulberries, grapes and cherries are used to make thick syrups, which, diluted with water and ice, are transformed into refreshing fruity or floral sherbet drinks. Sherbets (a word derived from the Arabic *shariba*, meaning 'to drink') are the most popular drinks of all, enjoyed throughout the day, and are available in public baths and cafés as well as in most traditional homes.

Serves 4–6

1 litre/1³/₄ pints/4 cups whole milk

50g/2oz/¹/₂ cup rice flour

125g/4¹/₄oz/²/₃ cup sugar

1–2 mastic crystals, pulverized with a little sugar

15–30ml/1–2 tbsp icing (confectioners') sugar, for dusting

Cook's tip Mastic can be found in Middle Eastern food stores; it is sold in the form of crystals, which need to be broken down with a mortar and pestle before using.

Milk pudding with mastic
Mouhalabieh

Middle Eastern milk puddings are absolutely delectable. Some are flavoured with orange blossom water, others with rose water, cinnamon or aniseed. Mastic, the crystallized gum from a small evergreen tree, gives the traditional milk pudding a unique resinous taste as well as a mildly chewy texture.

1 Mix the rice flour with a little of the milk to form a loose paste. Pour the rest of the milk into a heavy pan and stir in the sugar. Bring the milk to boiling point, stirring all the time, until the sugar has dissolved. Reduce the heat and stir a spoonful or two of the hot milk into the rice flour paste, then transfer the mixture into the pan, stirring constantly to avoid lumps.

2 Bring the milk back to boiling point and stir in the ground mastic. Reduce the heat and simmer gently for 20–25 minutes, stirring from time to time, until the mixture becomes quite thick and coats the back of the spoon.

3 Pour the mixture into serving bowls and let it cool, allowing a skin to form on top. Chill in the refrigerator and, just before serving, dust the tops with icing sugar.

Energy 239kcal/1006kJ; Protein 6g; Carbohydrate 40.8g, of which sugars 34.1g; Fat 6.6g, of which saturates 4g; Cholesterol 23mg; Calcium 207mg; Fibre 0.2g; Sodium 94mg

Spiced ground rice pudding
Moughli

This ground rice pudding is grainier than the traditional smooth milk puddings such as ashtalieh and mouhalabieh. Flavoured with cinnamon, which is regarded as beneficial and soothing to the health, moughli is traditionally served in Lebanon to women who have just given birth.

1 Pour 1.2 litres/2 pints/5 cups water into a heavy pan and bring it to the boil. Reduce the heat and beat in the ground rice, sugar and spices, stirring constantly to make sure the mixture is well blended and smooth. Simmer gently for about 15 minutes, until the mixture is very thick.

2 Transfer the mixture into individual serving bowls and leave to cool and set, then chill in the refrigerator.

3 When ready to serve, top each pudding with a sprinkling of coconut and pistachio nuts and eat chilled or at room temperature.

Energy 525kcal/2219kJ; Protein 5.1g; Carbohydrate 119.4g, of which sugars 78.8g; Fat 5g, of which saturates 2.9g; Cholesterol 0mg; Calcium 56mg; Fibre 0.8g; Sodium 20mg

Variation For extra flavour and crunch you could lightly dry roast the pistachio nuts and desiccated coconut. Let them cool before sprinkling on top of the pudding.

Serves 6

300g/11oz/scant 2 cups ground rice

450g/1lb/2¼ cups sugar

30ml/2 tbsp ground cinnamon

10ml/2 tsp ground aniseed

30ml/2 tbsp desiccated (dry unsweetened shredded) coconut

15ml/1 tbsp pistachio nuts, chopped

Cream cheese pudding with syrup and nuts
Ashtalieh

This cream cheese pudding is similar to the classic milk pudding, although thicker and creamier so that it can be cut into squares, which are then bathed in the traditional sugar syrup, kater. The pudding is invariably decorated with chopped pistachio nuts, almonds and pine nuts, which are soaked overnight to soften and refresh them.

Serves 4–6

1 litre/1³/₄ pints/4 cups full-fat milk

60ml/4 tbsp sugar

250g/9oz/generous 1 cup cream cheese

90ml/6 tbsp rice flour or cornflour (cornstarch), mixed with a little extra milk

10–15ml/2–3 tsp orange blossom water

15ml/1 tbsp pine nuts, soaked in cold water overnight

30ml/2 tbsp blanched almonds, soaked in cold water overnight and cut into slivers

30ml/2 tbsp pistachio nuts, chopped

For the syrup

225g/8oz/1 generous cup sugar

juice of 1 lemon

rind of ¹/₂ lemon, cut into fine strips

1 Heat the milk in a heavy pan with the sugar, stirring all the time, and bring it to the boil. Reduce the heat and add the cream cheese, beating it into the milk and sugar until the mixture is smooth.

2 Add a couple of spoonfuls of the hot mixture to the slaked rice flour, then pour it into the pan, whisking vigorously until the mixture thickens.

3 Stir in the orange blossom water, and simmer gently for 10–15 minutes until it is very thick. Pour the mixture into a shallow dish and leave it to cool and set. Chill in the refrigerator until ready to use.

4 To make the syrup, put the sugar in a heavy-based pan with 120ml/4fl oz/¹/₂ cup water and bring it to the boil, stirring constantly until the sugar has dissolved.

5 Add the lemon juice and rind, reduce the heat and simmer for 10 minutes, until the syrup is thick enough to coat the back of a spoon. Remove from the heat and leave the syrup to cool.

6 When ready to serve, divide the pudding into squares and place them on individual plates. Spoon some of the syrup over them and decorate with the nuts. Serve chilled or at room temperature.

Energy 613kcal/2561kJ; Protein 10.1g; Carbohydrate 70.5g, of which sugars 58.2g; Fat 33.7g, of which saturates 17.1g; Cholesterol 63mg; Calcium 279mg; Fibre 1g; Sodium 248mg

Sweet turmeric cakes
Sfouf

Light and spongy with a distinctive colour and flavouring from the turmeric, these rustic cakes are a feature of the mountain villages of Lebanon, where they are served for breakfast, or to accompany a mid-morning coffee or tea.

1 Preheat the oven to 180°C/350°F/Gas 4. Smear the tahini over the base and sides of a 25 x 20cm/10 x 8in baking tin (pan). Sift together the semolina, flour, baking powder and turmeric on to baking parchment or into a bowl and set aside.

2 Heat the milk with the sugar in a heavy pan, stirring constantly, until almost boiling. Melt the butter with the olive oil in a separate pan, then stir it into the milk.

3 Add the semolina and flour mixture into the milk and beat vigorously to make a smooth batter. Pour the batter into the prepared tin, sprinkle the surface with pine nuts and bake in the oven for about 30 minutes.

4 Remove the cake from the oven and leave to cool, then cut it into 5cm/2in squares and serve while still warm, or at room temperature.

Energy 624kcal/2632kJ; Protein 11.4g; Carbohydrate 106.2g, of which sugars 46.8g; Fat 20.2g, of which saturates 4.6g; Cholesterol 13mg; Calcium 164mg; Fibre 2.2g; Sodium 70mg

Serves 4–6

15–30ml/1–2 tbsp tahini

250g/9oz/1½ cups semolina

200g/7oz/1¾ cups plain (all-purpose) flour

10ml/2 tsp baking powder

30ml/2 tbsp ground turmeric

350ml/12fl oz/1½ cups milk

250g/9oz/1¼ cups sugar

25g/1oz/2 tbsp butter

75ml/5 tbsp olive oil

30ml/2 tbsp pine nuts

Serves 6–8

115g/4oz/¹/₂ cup butter

175g/6oz/scant 1 cup sugar

30–45ml/2–3 tbsp white or blue poppy seeds

5–10ml/1–2 tsp vanilla extract

2 eggs

450g/1lb/2²/₃ cups fine semolina

5ml/1 tsp baking powder

2.5ml/¹/₂ tsp bicarbonate of soda (baking soda)

175g/6fl oz/³/₄ cup strained yogurt

16 blanched almonds, halved

For the syrup

250ml/8fl oz/1 cup water

450g/1lb/2¹/₄ cups sugar

juice of 1 lemon

Semolina cake with poppy seeds
Basbousa

Poppy seed cakes are particularly enjoyed by the Jewish community of Lebanon, who prepare them for the festival of Purim. Blue poppy seeds give the cakes a pretty speckled look, or you can use white poppy seeds.

1 First make the syrup. Boil the water with the sugar, stirring constantly, until dissolved. Stir in the lemon juice, reduce the heat and simmer for 10–15 minutes, until the syrup coats the back of a wooden spoon. Leave the syrup to cool.

2 Preheat the oven to 180°C/350°F/Gas 4 and grease a 20 x 30cm/8 x 12in baking tin (pan). Cream the butter with the sugar, beat in the poppy seeds and vanilla and add the eggs one at a time. Sift the semolina with the baking powder and bicarbonate of soda and fold it into the creamed mixture with the yogurt.

3 Turn the mixture into the prepared tin, spreading it evenly to the edges. Place the almonds on top, arranged in lines, and bake for about 30 minutes, or until a skewer inserted comes out clean. Pour the syrup over the hot cake. Cut the cake into diamonds and return to the oven for 5 minutes to create a sticky top.

Energy 664kcal/2809kJ; Protein 9.9g; Carbohydrate 127g, of which sugars 83.4g; Fat 16.5g, of which saturates 8.5g; Cholesterol 81mg; Calcium 120mg; Fibre 1.5g; Sodium 156mg

Nights of Lebanon
Layali loubnan

This is a popular layered pudding that can be prepared ahead of time and is often made for feasts and family celebrations. Traditionally, it has a layer of semolina, followed by a layer of kashta (a scented creamy mixture), topped by a layer of bananas, and finished with nuts, but it can include additional ingredients, such as apricot, cherry or rose petal conserves, or even tahini. The whole pudding is drizzled in amber honey and orange blossom water.

1 First prepare the semolina. Heat the milk with the sugar in a heavy pan, stirring until the sugar has dissolved. Bring the milk to the boil, then add in the semolina and the mastic, beating vigorously. Reduce the heat and simmer, stirring from time to time, until the mixture begins to thicken. Pour it into a serving dish, level it with the back of a spoon and leave to cool.

2 To prepare the cream layer, mix the rice flour with a little milk, heat the rest of the milk and cream, together with the sugar, stirring constantly, until almost boiling. Stir a spoonful of the hot mixture into the rice flour mixture and then pour the rice flour mixture back into the pan.

3 Add the breadcrumbs and rose water to the pan and stir vigorously until the mixture is thick and creamy. Leave to cool a little, then spoon it over the semolina, which should have set. Leave to cool and set, then chill the pudding.

4 A little time before serving, arrange the sliced bananas in a layer over the pudding. Squeeze lemon juice over the top to prevent them from turning brown. Sprinkle the nuts on top. Heat the honey with the orange blossom water and pour it over the nuts. Once the honey has cooled, chill the pudding until ready to eat.

Energy 431kcal/1799kJ; Protein 7.5g; Carbohydrate 43.5g, of which sugars 27.8g; Fat 28.4g, of which saturates 14g; Cholesterol 62mg; Calcium 158mg; Fibre 1.2g; Sodium 124mg

Above: A waiter pours coffee at the dessert table of a Beirut restaurant.

Serves 6–8

For the semolina

600ml/1 pint/2¹/₂ cups whole milk

60ml/4 tbsp sugar

90g/3¹/₂oz/¹/₂ cup fine semolina

1–2 mastic crystals, pulverized with a little sugar

For the cream

15ml/1 tbsp rice flour

150ml/¹/₄ pint/²/₃ cup whole milk

300ml/¹/₂ pint/1¹/₄ cups double (heavy) cream

30–45ml/2–3 tbsp sugar

2 slices white bread, ground to crumbs

15ml/1 tbsp rose water

For the topping

2 bananas, finely sliced

juice of ¹/₂ lemon

30ml/2 tbsp chopped pistachio nuts

30ml/2 tbsp flaked almonds

45–60ml/3–4 tbsp fragrant runny honey

30ml/2 tbsp orange blossom water

Puffed fritters in syrup
Awamat

Lebanese Christians prepare awamat on 6 January to celebrate the baptism of Christ. The tradition of eating golden fritters bathed in syrup to celebrate religious occasions dates back to the medieval feasts of Baghdad and, later, to the lavish banquets of the Ottoman Empire.

Serves 6

2.5ml/¹/₂ tsp dried yeast

2.5ml/¹/₂ tsp sugar

150ml/¹/₄ pint/²/₃ cup lukewarm water

175g/6oz/1¹/₂ cups plain (all-purpose) flour

50g/2oz/¹/₂ cup rice flour

1–2 mastic crystals, pulverized with 5ml/1 tsp sugar

sunflower oil, for frying

pinch of salt

For the syrup

225g/8oz/1 cup sugar

150ml/¹/₄ pint/²/₃ cup water

30ml/2 tbsp orange blossom water

1 In a small bowl, cream the yeast with the sugar in the lukewarm water, until frothy. Sift the flours with the salt and mastic into a bowl and make a well in the centre. Pour the creamed yeast into the well and draw in a little of the flour to form a batter. Dust the surface of the batter with a little of the remaining flour, cover the bowl with a clean damp cloth, and leave the batter to sponge for about 20 minutes.

2 Remove the cloth and draw in the rest of the flour to make a soft, sticky dough, adding a little extra water if necessary. Cover the bowl with the damp cloth again and leave the dough to prove for about 2 hours, until doubled in size.

3 Meanwhile, prepare the syrup. Place the sugar and water in a heavy pan and bring it to the boil, stirring constantly. Stir in the orange blossom water, reduce the heat and simmer for about 10 minutes, until the syrup coats the back of a wooden spoon. Turn off the heat and leave the syrup to cool.

4 Heat enough sunflower oil in a pan for frying. Take a portion of the dough in your hand and squeeze it through thumb and forefinger to drop little balls of dough into the oil. Alternatively, use a teaspoon – the shapes do not need to be perfect.

5 Fry the fritters in batches until golden brown and drain on kitchen paper. While still warm, soak the fritters in the cold syrup for 10–15 minutes. Scoop them out and serve at room temperature with a little of the syrup drizzled over them.

Energy 193kcal/806kJ; Protein 4.1g; Carbohydrate 30.9g, of which sugars 11.5g; Fat 6.6g, of which saturates 0.5g; Cholesterol 0mg; Calcium 23mg; Fibre 0.6g; Sodium 3mg

Serves 6

225g/8oz/1¼ cups whole wheat grains, soaked overnight and drained

1 litre/1¾ pints/4 cups water

60–90ml/4–6 tbsp fragrant runny honey

30ml/2 tbsp orange blossom water

30ml/2 tbsp rose water

30–45ml/2–3 tbsp raisins or sultanas (golden raisins), soaked in warm water for 30 minutes and drained

30ml/2 tbsp pine nuts, soaked in water for 2 hours

30ml/2 tbsp blanched almonds, soaked in water for 2 hours

seeds of ½ pomegranate

Wheat in fragrant honey
Kamhiyeh

In Lebanon, this simple dessert is traditionally prepared with young green wheat or barley to mark significant events. For Muslims, it is a dish prepared for nursing mothers; Jews serve it to celebrate a baby's first tooth; and for Christians, it is eaten on 4 December in honour of St Barbara.

1 Place the whole wheat grains in a heavy pan with the water and bring to the boil. Reduce the heat, cover, and simmer for about 1 hour, until the grains are tender and most of the water has been absorbed.

2 Meanwhile, heat the honey and stir in the orange blossom and rose waters – don't let it bubble up. Stir in the raisins and turn off the heat.

3 Transfer the wheat grains into a serving bowl, or individual bowls, and pour the honey and raisins over the top. Garnish with the nuts and pomegranate seeds and serve while still warm, or leave to cool and chill in the refrigerator before serving.

Energy 193kcal/806kJ; Protein 4.1g; Carbohydrate 30.9g, of which sugars 11.5g; Fat 6.6g, of which saturates 0.5g; Cholesterol 0mg; Calcium 23mg; Fibre 0.6g; Sodium 3mg

Pomegranate salad with pine nuts and honey
Salatet al rumman

Variations of this pretty, decorative salad are prepared throughout the Middle East. It can be offered to guests as a mark of hospitality, or it can be served as a refreshing dish between courses, at the end of a meal, and as an accompaniment to other sweet dishes.

1 Place the pine nuts in a bowl, cover with the water and leave for 2 hours.

2 Cut the pomegranates into quarters on a plate so that you catch the juice. Extract the seeds, taking care to discard the bitter pith and membrane, and place in a bowl with the juice. Drain the pine nuts and add them to the bowl.

3 Stir in the orange blossom water and honey, cover the bowl, and chill in the refrigerator. Serve chilled, or at room temperature, decorated with mint leaves.

Energy 82kcal/344kJ; Protein 1.3g; Carbohydrate 8.2g, of which sugars 8.1g; Fat 5.2g, of which saturates 0.4g; Cholesterol 0mg; Calcium 4mg; Fibre 1.2g; Sodium 2mg

Serves 4–6

45–60ml/3–4 tbsp pine nuts

3 ripe pomegranates

30ml/2 tbsp orange blossom water

15–30ml/1–2 tbsp fragrant runny honey

handful of small mint leaves, to decorate

Cook's tip Pomegranates signify good luck and prosperity, which is why they are served to welcome visitors to the home.

Stuffed red date preserve
Mrabba al-balah

This is a beautiful and unusual preserve, revered in Lebanon and Jordan. Dates are one of the region's most ancient staple foods, coveted for their nutritional value and their sweetness. It is said that the Bedouin cannot sleep under fruit-laden date palms, such is their urge to pick and devour the fruit.

1 Place the dates in a heavy pan and just cover with water. Bring to the boil, reduce the heat and simmer for 5 minutes to soften the dates. Drain the dates, reserving the water, and carefully push the stone (pit) out of each date with a skewer or a sharp knife. Stuff each date with an almond.

2 Pour the reserved cooking water back into the pan and add the sugar, clementine juice and rind, and the cloves. Bring the water to the boil, stirring constantly until the sugar has dissolved.

3 Reduce the heat and drop in the stuffed dates. Simmer for about 1 hour, until the syrup is fairly thick. Leave the dates to cool in the syrup, then spoon them into jars to enjoy with bread, yogurt, milk puddings, or just as a treat on their own.

Energy 1619kcal/6871kJ; Protein 15.8g; Carbohydrate 347.4g, of which sugars 346g; Fat 28.2g, of which saturates 2.4g; Cholesterol 0mg; Calcium 318mg; Fibre 8.3g; Sodium 45mg

Makes enough for 2 x 450g/1lb jars

40 fresh, ripe red dates

40 blanched whole almonds

500g/1¼lb/2½ cups sugar

juice and rind (cut into fine strips) of 2 clementines

6–8 cloves

Makes enough for 3–4 x 1lb jars

1kg/2¼lb fresh quinces, peeled (optional), quartered, cored and diced

juice of 2 lemons

500g/1¼lb/2½ cups sugar

Quince preserve
Mrabba al-safarjal

Many delectable jams and syrups are made in the eastern Mediterranean, but in Lebanon quince jam is particularly sought after as the fragrant fruit is associated with love and marriage. More of a conserve than a spreadable jam, this quince preserve is best spooned generously on to freshly baked bread, or drizzled over yogurt.

1 Place the prepared fruit in a heavy pan and sprinkle with the lemon juice to prevent it from turning brown. Pour in about 600ml/1 pint/2½ cups water – just enough to surround the fruit – and add the sugar.

2 Bring to the boil, stirring constantly until the sugar dissolves. Reduce the heat and simmer for 1–1½ hours, until the fruit has turned a deep reddish-pink. Turn up the heat and boil vigorously for 2 minutes, then spoon the mixture into sterilized jars. Seal and store in a cool place for at least 6 months, if not eating immediately.

Energy 593kcal/2524kJ; Protein 1.4g; Carbohydrate 155.6g, of which sugars 155.6g; Fat 0.3g, of which saturates 0g; Cholesterol 0mg; Calcium 94mg; Fibre 5.5g; Sodium 15mg

Serves 2

20ml/4 heaped tsp finely ground coffee

seeds of 2–3 cardamom pods, ground

10ml/2 tsp sugar, or more to taste

Lebanese coffee with cardamom
Kahwe Lebananieh

Lebanese coffee is very similar to the better-known Turkish coffee, although it is traditionally flavoured with cardamom. You can buy the finely ground coffee required to make it in Middle Eastern stores and some delicatessens. It is prepared in a distinctive long-handled pot, known as a *rakweh* in Lebanon, and is generally served black and already sweetened.

1 Put two coffee-cupfuls of water into the rakweh, or a small pot, and heap the coffee, cardamom and sugar on the surface. Place on the heat. As the water begins to boil, stir the coffee into the water. Allow to bubble for 2–3 minutes, stirring constantly, then pour the coffee into the cups.

2 Serve immediately, but let the coffee sit for a moment before drinking, so that the grounds sink to the bottom of the cup.

Energy 22kcal/92kJ; Protein 0.3g; Carbohydrate 5.5g, of which sugars 5.2g; Fat 0g, of which saturates 0g; Cholesterol 0mg; Calcium 6mg; Fibre 0g; Sodium 1mg

Cook's tip To grind the cardamom pods, simply crush the pods in a mortar and pestle, or on a wooden board with the flat side of a heavy, bladed knife. You want to split them rather than grind them to dust.

Rose water sherbet
Sharab al ward

A deliciously fragrant drink with an air of antiquity and elegance, this rose water sherbet is often served in sophisticated surroundings in Lebanon. It is a drink of hospitality and celebration.

1 Put the sugar and water into a heavy-based pan and bring it to the boil, stirring constantly until the sugar has dissolved. Stir in the lemon juice and rose water and reduce the heat. Simmer gently for 15–20 minutes, until the syrup is thick and coats the back of a wooden spoon.

2 If using food colouring, stir in a few drops to turn the syrup rose pink. Leave to cool in the pan, then pour it into a sterilized bottle and store in a cool place.

3 When ready to serve a glass of sherbet, drop several ice cubes into a stylish glass and leave it in the freezer for a while to frost the sides. Pour 15–30ml/1–2 tbsp (or more if you like) of the syrup into the glass and dilute to taste with cold water. Garnish with rose petals or a slice of lemon and serve immediately.

Energy 1981kcal/8455kJ; Protein 3g; Carbohydrate 525.1g, of which sugars 525.1g; Fat 0g, of which saturates 0g; Cholesterol 0mg; Calcium 276mg; Fibre 0.2g; Sodium 32mg

Makes 900ml/1¹/₂ pints/3³/₄ cups

500g/1¹/₄lb/2¹/₂ cups sugar

250ml/8fl oz/1 cup water

juice of ¹/₂ lemon

150ml/¹/₄ pint/²/₃ cup rose water

red food colouring (optional)

fresh fragrant rose petals or a slice of lemon, to decorate

Useful addresses

Australia

Lebanese Patisserie
(wholesaler specializing in cakes, pastries and fresh bread)
Unit 3/173 Camboon Road
Malaga, Western Australia 6090
Tel: +61 08 9249 1644
www.lebanesepatisserie.com.au

Harkola
(Lebanese food specialist)
3–7 Highgate Street
Auburn, New South Wales 2144
Tel: +61 02 9737 8883
www.harkola.com/food-wholesaler.asp

Sydney Road, Brunswick
(street full of shops stocking the basics of Middle Eastern cuisine)

Middle East Bakeries
(supplies range of Middle Eastern breads and groceries)
20 Hope Street, Brunswick
Tel: (03) 9388 1044

New Zealand

The Pita House
(Middle Eastern food store)
277a Neilson Street
Onehunga, Auckland 1061
Tel: 01 64 9636 2005
Email: pitahouse@xtra.co.nz

Sahara Foods
(produces Middle Eastern organic dips and spreads)
39 Waterman Place, Ferrymead, Christchurch,
New Zealand 8023
Tel: 01 64 3384 6438
www.sahara.co.nz

Canada

Lordia
(restaurant featuring authentic Lebanese cuisine)
3883 Perron Boulevard
Laval, Quebec,
H7V 1P8
Tel: +1 450 681 9999
www.lordia.com

Kiki Lebanese Food and Bakery
2045 Meadowbrook Rd
Gloucester, Ontario,
K1B 4W7
Tel: +1 613 746 9988

Mid-East Food Centre
(supplier of Middle Eastern ingredients and delicacies)
2595 Agricola St.
Halifax, Nova Scotia,
B3K 4C4
Tel: +1 902 492 0958

Masri Sweets
(prepares a line of Arabic pastries for online ordering)
6235 Schaefer Rd
Dearborn, Mi 48126
Tel: +1 313 584 3500
info@masrisweets.com

United States

Buylebanese.com
(online supermarket)
Tel: 001 (961) 360 2405
www.buylebanese.com

Lebanese Food Market
564 Hancock Street
Quincy, Massachusetts 02169
Tel: 001 (617) 699-5887

Lebanese Taverna
(public and private cooking classes)
4400 Old Dominion Drive
Arlington,
Virginia 22207
Tel: 001 (703) 276-8681

Mama's Bakery and Lebanese Deli
4237 Alabama Street
San Diego,
California 92104
Tel: 001 (619) 688-0717

St. Anthony-St. George Maronite Parish
(holds an annual food fair in November with a wide range of Lebanese ingredients)
79 Loomis Street
Wilkes-Barre,
Pennsylvania 18702
Tel: 001 (570) 824-3599
stanthonystgeorge@yahoo.com

United Kingdom

The Arabica Food & Spice Company
(wholesaler of Lebanese pastes, pickles and preserves)
Arch 257 Grosvenor Court
London,
SE5 0NP
Tel: 020 7708 5577
www.arabicafoodandspice.com

Noura Belgravia
(restaurant specialising in Lebanese cuisine)
16 Hobart Place
London, SW1 0HH
Tel: 020 7235 9444
www.noura.co.uk

The publishers would like to thank the following agencies for the use of their images:

Alamy: pp7 (both), 8, 9tr, 10 (both), 11 (both), 12 (both), 13, 15bl, 16tl, 21t, 79m, 83tr, 121m, 124tl, 141m & 151tr.
Corbis: pp9tl, 16tr, 21b, 109tr.
Getty Images: pp14, 16b, 41m, 45tr, 48tl, 54tl, 57tr, 63m, 67tr, 91tr, 97m, 100tl.

Index